GROWN-UP GIRLFRIENDS

Finding and Keeping
Real Friends in the Real World

ERIN SMALLEY
AND CARRIE OLIVER

TYNDALE HOUSE PUBLISHERS, INC.
CAROL STREAM, ILLINOIS

5.17.0?
FR Terry

Visit Tyndale's exciting Web site at www.tyndale.com

TYNDALE and Tyndale's quill logo are registered trademarks of Tyndale House Publishers, Inc.

Focus on the Family is a registered trademark of Focus on the Family, Colorado Springs, Colorado.

Grown-Up Girlfriends: Finding and Keeping Real Friends in the Real World

Copyright © 2007 by Erin Smalley and Carrie Oliver. All rights reserved.

Cover photo of yellow purse copyright © by Louis Aguinaldo/iStockphoto.com. All rights reserved.

Cover photo of green purse copyright © by Rosmizan Abu Seman/Dreamstime. All rights reserved.

Authors' photo taken in 2006.

Designed by Beth Sparkman

Edited by Kimberly Miller

To protect the privacy of individuals, some names and details have been changed in the stories that appear in this book.

Published in association with the literary agency of Alive Communications, Inc., 7680 Goddard Street, Suite 200, Colorado Springs, CO 80920.

Unless otherwise indicated, Scripture quotations are taken from the *Holy Bible,* New International Version®. NIV®. Copyright © 1973, 1978, 1984 by International Bible Society. Used by permission of Zondervan. All rights reserved.

Scripture quotations marked NASB are taken from the NEW AMERICAN STANDARD BIBLE®, Copyright © 1960, 1962, 1963, 1968, 1971, 1972, 1973, 1975, 1977, 1995 by The Lockman Foundation. Used by permission.

Scripture quotations marked NKJV™ taken from the New King James Version.® Copyright © 1982 by Thomas Nelson, Inc. Used by permission. All rights reserved.

Scripture quotations marked KJV are taken from the *Holy Bible,* King James Version.

Scripture quotations marked *"THE MESSAGE"* are taken from *THE MESSAGE* paraphrase. Copyright © by Eugene H. Peterson 1993, 1994, 1995, 1996, 2000, 2001, 2002. Used by permission of NavPress Publishing Group.

Scripture quotations marked TLB are taken from *The Living Bible* paraphrase copyright © 1971. Used by permission of Tyndale House Publishers, Inc., Carol Stream, Illinois 60188. All rights reserved.

Library of Congress Cataloging-in-Publication Data

Smalley, Erin
    Grown-up girlfriends : finding and keeping real friends in the real world / Erin Smalley and Carrie Oliver.
        p. cm.
    Includes bibliographical references (p.   ).
    ISBN-13: 978-1-4143-0809-8 (sc)
    ISBN-10: 1-4143-0809-4 (sc)
    1. Christian women—Religious life. 2. Female friendship—Religious aspects—Christianity. I. Oliver, Carrie, date. II. Title
    BV 4527. S56 2007
    241'.6762082—dc22   2006034394

Printed in the United States of America

13   12   11   10   09   08   07
7   6   5   4   3   2

DEDICATION

This book is dedicated to
my amazing husband, Greg;
my dear children, Taylor, Madalyn, and Garrison;
and
my first friend in life, my mom,
Rosalie Antoinette Murphy.

Erin Smalley

To my family—husband, Gary;
Nathan and his wife, Amy;
Matt and his fiancée, Amanda; and Andrew.
You have supported me, loved me, and encouraged me to keep
going, even on the days when I was pretty sure I couldn't do this!
You are royalty in my life, and you give gifts of gold with
each of your precious hearts.

Carrie Oliver

CONTENTS

Acknowledgments

I'd like to first and foremost thank my Lord, who prompted the writing of this book more than five years ago. He has been faithful to create the time and energy for this project during various challenging circumstances.

Thank you to all the girlfriends, old and new, who have been patient and loving enough to teach me what being a "grown-up girlfriend" means. As I have lived in many places, thank you to the girlfriends who truly made it feel like "home" in Arizona, Colorado, California, Missouri, and Arkansas. I wish I could include all of you by name and truly describe the treasures you are to me, but no words could convey the love and gratefulness I have for each of you. Thank you to the friends who have held my hand and not let go through "real life."

Thank you to Lisa Johnson, Nancy Breaux, and Janet Fritsch, who have been my cheerleaders with writing and speaking for more than five years. Your friendship is priceless and your encouragement a gift.

Thank you, Carrie Oliver, for your willingness to write with me. Your strength has forever touched my life.

Thank you to my parents. Mom, you have given me constant strength. I am so grateful God chose you both to be my parents—my life would have been so different without your guidance and love.

Thank you to my mother-in-law, Norma Smalley, for talking to me long ago on that porch swing and trusting me with your son. To Kari, my sister-in-love, thank you for my bracelet and all that it represents. Thanks to Amy and Selena—for becoming like sisters to me over the years.

Thank you to my husband, Greg, whom I love more today than I ever thought possible. You have been God's greatest gift in my life. I wouldn't be who I am today without you, and this book would never have been completed without your guidance and direction. Your constant love and encouragement are true blessings. And lastly, to Taylor, Maddy, and Garrison—being your mom is the greatest privilege in my life. I am in constant awe that I get to be your mom—I love you to the moon and back!

I would also like to thank my agent, Lee Hough, at Alive Communications for his constant insight and support in bringing this project into reality. Thank you to Tyndale House Publishers—especially Doug Knox, Jan Long Harris, Nancy Clausen, Sharon Leavitt, Stephanie Voiland, and Beth Sparkman—for your support and for believing in us. Thank you to Focus on the Family for taking this project on and being committed to it.

Thank you to our editor, Kim Miller. You have been such a joy to work with. Your tenderness and gentleness with suggestions and changes have been priceless. You truly took this project to a whole new level. Thank you for all the tireless hours you gave to this book. You have truly been a blessing.

Erin Smalley

I thank my dear Lord Jesus Christ, who carried me and gave me the faith, hope, and strength to walk through this disease to focus and write and give of my heart and life. Erin Smalley, your invitation to write on friendship together was not only a great idea but also a gift to me. I will never forget your call several years ago when you asked me to help write a book with you on friendship. I said yes, but I really meant, "Yeah, right!" We both know what Jesus can do when He wants something done!

To my mother, Marilyn, and my two sisters, Chris and Barb, as you have been more than family but dear friends to me throughout a lifetime. I continue to treasure you all and every moment we capture together. Sweet, sweet Marsha, you are my sister-in-law but a sister in the truest sense, and I love you for your fervent prayers and almost daily calls.

As I have walked through life, lived in several places, and battled cancer for the last year and a half, I want to thank you, dear friends, whom God has used to teach me what friendship really looks like. Every single one of you has held my heart and loved me well. This book could not have been written without your prayers, your love, your encouragement and support, your understanding, your witness in my life, and the relationship experiences you gave to me. I am honored and humbled to call each of you friend. There are not enough pages to write your names and say all the things I want to say, so just know that my heart would do that if I could and feel my gratitude for you and my hugs to you all.

Thank you, Tyndale and Focus on the Family, for your willingness to partner with Erin and me and work with us in a loving and professional manner. Kim Miller, you are the editor straight from heaven, and my thankfulness for you is great. Thanks to you, Lee Hough, for your professionalism and continued support and help as we carved out this project. It is done!

Carrie Oliver

$\mathcal{I}$NTRODUCTION

Erin

I clearly remember the day five years ago when I first felt a deep desire to write a book on female friendships. I was sitting in a Sam's Club parking lot, resting my arm against my very pregnant belly while eating a chocolate donut. For several days I'd been struggling with my desire to be "all things to all friends" while also trying to guide my first-grade daughter through her first friendship crisis.

I called my mentor-friend, Carrie Oliver, and asked her if she would join me in writing a book on female friendships. Immediately she agreed. We knew right away that we wanted to help women discover how to form the kind of deep, purposeful relationships that meet our longing for connection and make a difference in the lives of others.

Can I let you in on a little secret as we get started? Not all friendships are meant to be deep and intimate. Nor will you instantly bond with every—even most—new women you meet. In this book, we discuss the different types of friendships and offer some guidelines on how to determine which friends it's worth trying to go deeper with.

Friendships can provide both mountaintop experiences and painful valleys. In this book we discuss both. Our desire is not to learn how to hide the pain or to take the difficulties away, but to learn how to grow through the difficult times in a more effective and healthy manner—one that is honoring to the Lord, others, and also ourselves.

My friendships have taken on a new importance while I've been navigating the stresses of the past year. Our family has just moved twice in Siloam Springs, Arkansas—once into a rental house and then into a more permanent home. We are adjusting to living in a new community (our seventh in fourteen years of marriage), and my husband is settling into a new career as a professor at John Brown University. However, the most challenging part for me over the past six months has been dealing with cancer. My mom was diagnosed with lung cancer in January 2006, and my dear coauthor, Carrie, is fighting pancreatic cancer. Again, the Lord is teaching me about new aspects of friendship—of loving two women with cancer, dealing with my own grief, and allowing Him to bring others into my life to minister to me in the midst of such pain.

However, the bottom line is that five years ago the Lord knew this would be my world right now. In the midst of all of this, He has provided me with an overwhelming amount of support—some wonderful new friends and many long-standing "soul mate" friends.

I pray that He will use this book, as He has used these experiences in my life, to ultimately draw you closer to Him. Together let's join in this journey of learning about being a "grown-up" friend.

May your friendships be blessed in a mighty way.

Carrie

Over the years, I've seen God use friends to mold me, shape me, and help me become more like Himself. I believe He has used me in the lives of my friends as well. Yet I have never experienced the powerful force and working of friendship in my life more than in the past year.

As Erin mentioned, I am in the battle of my life. I was diagnosed with cancer in May 2005. I am still here with a mission in my life: to write this book, to heal, to look more like Christ with each day, and to love my friends as they have loved me. I have learned so much about friendship, purpose, God's hand, forgiveness, laughter, kindness, support, connectedness, and prayer on this cancer journey.

I remember the day Erin called to suggest we write a book together on friendship. I was sitting at home in my husband's office paying bills. I was glad to hear from Erin, and I said something profound like, "Sure, that would be fun!" Little did I know the journey God would be taking us on as He prepared us to write this book over a period of five years.

This book includes many lessons I've learned—both through my walk with friends and my times with clients in my counseling office. It also reflects the personal lessons I've learned through my failures, weaknesses, and difficult times.

When Erin and I began to actually talk about writing this book, we asked ourselves, "So why another book on friendship?" What was driving us to focus on friendships, and what could we possibly offer from our own experiences that might impact you, the reader, in your life and your friendships? Before long, we realized that our aim was to write about the uniqueness of a "grown-up" friendship, which stretches and encourages both women. Growing up means that we develop, mature, and become wiser, taking on the fruit of the Spirit and the character of Christ. It means we "put away childish things" (1 Corinthians 13:11, NKJV). So what does a grown-up friendship look like? We'll address that question in chapter 2.

I don't know about you, but I know that I have not always looked very "adult" in my friendships! At times I have been fearful of conflict, I have been jealous, I have expected too much, I have been harsh and unkind. Yep, at times I have acted like a selfish child who needed some help growing up. I also have had friends who were not grown up with me. I have been shunned, lied to, rejected, not thought the best of, devalued, betrayed, and gossiped about. Just like so many other relationships, such as marriage, parenthood, and work-related relationships, friendship requires effort, intentionality, prayer, understanding, and a desire for God to be at the center.

This book not only discusses how you can establish healthy friendships, it also helps you identify those relationships that could be potentially destructive. We talk about different types of friendships, acknowledging that not all friendships are meant to be deep and intimate. As we grow up we can better discern who God is calling us to be more intimate with, especially as we understand the purpose of the relationship.

As you read this book, my prayer is that God will become more real, more tangible, and more intimate to you, that you will be encouraged to experience friendship with greater purpose and a fresh passion. I love what Henri Nouwen, in his book *The Inner Voice of Love*, says about the meaning of friendship:

> *God is faithful to God's promises. Before you die, you will find the acceptance and the love you crave. It will not come in the way you expect. It will not follow your needs and wishes. But it will fill your heart and satisfy your deepest desire.*[1]

Blessings to you!

1

THE STORY OF TWO FRIENDSHIP BRACELETS

[Erin]

Everything in life that truly matters can be boiled down to relationships.
—Gary Smalley, THE DNA OF RELATIONSHIPS

I have two friendship bracelets. One is a treasured gift from a close friend, and I wear it almost every day.

The other is decades old but has never been worn. When I stumbled across it again in my closet a few years ago, the small gift-wrapped jewelry box in which it rests was covered with dust. Amazingly, the wrapping paper was still in perfect condition—not a tear or rip anywhere. The colors, although somewhat faded, looked beautiful—hip, even. Groovy happy faces in purple, hot pink, yellow, and green patterns covered the gift. A small card still hung from the ribbon. A lump formed in my throat as I read the words:

Jenny,
Happy Birthday! I hope you enjoy your gift.
BFF (Best Friends Forever)!
Love, Erin

I couldn't believe I had held on to it for more than twenty years. Instantly, painful memories flooded my mind. *Jenny.* I hadn't thought about her for years. The party. I had tried to block it out. But here it was . . . the gift. Jenny's gift. I had forgotten that I never gave it to her.

In 1981 I was in seventh grade. My two best friends were Jenny Bower and Kelly Chavez. It's hard to describe our relationship exactly. Although the three of us were close, inevitably one of us would feel left out. We all seemed to strive to be the "queen bee"; you know, the leader of the pack—the most valued friend.

About the time I bought the bracelet, Jenny and I were going through a tough stretch. Apparently she felt that I was spending too much time with Kelly, and she felt left out. Jenny started ignoring me. Actually, she began giving me the silent treatment. Hurt, I began hanging out more with another friend named Glenda. Two opposing teams quickly formed: Jenny and Kelly on one side and Glenda and me on the other. Over the next week we gossiped about each other, ignored each other, and were just plain cruel. At the time, I had no idea why Jenny was upset with me. I figured it might be because Kelly and I had been walking to school together, most of the time without her. I tried to milk information out of Kelly—she would actually talk to me when we weren't in school—but she didn't seem to know why Jenny was upset either. And then it happened.

"Do you want to ride to the party together?" Kelly asked me over the phone.

Party? What party? I thought to myself.

"What are you talking about, Kelly?"

"You know . . . Jenny's birthday party."

I'm sure she could sense something was wrong. I didn't say anything—or breathe for that matter—for several long seconds.

"Jenny's having a birthday party?" I asked.

"I think so . . . yes . . . well, maybe," Kelly stammered. "Hey, let me call you back. My mom needs to use the phone." And the line went dead.

I couldn't believe what I had just heard. Jenny was having a birthday party, and I wasn't invited. I was devastated. I immediately grabbed the birthday present I had wrapped for her just the day before and threw it into my closet.

The next day at school I found out that eight girls from my class had been invited to Jenny's thirteenth birthday party. And I wasn't one of them. All because Jenny and I had been in a fight—the cause of which I never discovered. I cried so hard that weekend. I felt rejected, displaced, and unloved—new feelings for me.

Ironically, a week later Jenny and I were friends again. We never talked about the birthday party or why she had been mad at me. We pretended that nothing had happened.

The present I had bought her was a bracelet. On the bracelet was a friendship charm. I'm sure I was acting passive-aggressive, but after having felt so rejected, I never gave her my gift—I didn't feel she deserved to wear a BFF (Best Friends Forever) bracelet from me.

When I discovered the box again a few years ago, I carefully unwrapped it. As I held the "antique" bracelet in my hand, a tear rolled down my cheek. The pain I felt in my heart was as intense as it had been more than twenty years ago. Girls can be so cruel—especially at thirteen.

I'm grateful to have another friendship bracelet—though it, too, remained hidden in a box for years. This one came from my sister-in-law, one of my closest friends. She'd bought it for me at one of the high points of my life. I was about to marry the love of my life, and I was also going to become family with her—my dearest girlfriend! Who would have ever thought that I would end up marrying the brother of one of my best friends?

Kari and I had been friends since our sophomore year of college, when she'd reached out to me and helped me grow in my faith. We shared many of the same interests: jogging, eating sushi, and dating the same guy (at different times, of course!). One summer, she encouraged me to work with her at a Christian sports camp. Our friendship blossomed to a new level there, and we got to know and love one another even more. Before long I got to know her family—including her brother, Greg.

When Greg and I married, I had high expectations for the friendship between Kari and me. I dreamed of the years ahead when we would build our own households and raise our children together. I was sure we'd remain friends until we were old and gray.

But one week after Greg and I returned from our honeymoon, I could tell something was wrong. Kari didn't seem excited to see me. She was pretty quiet, and for the first time in my life, I didn't have anything to say either. When we did speak, it was simple small talk—definitely not the deep, intimate communication we had once shared. Over the next few months, the unspoken tension between us grew, and I soon began to fear that all my dreams of our friendship were going to disappear.

Looking back, I can see how difficult it must have been to be in Kari's shoes. Until I married Greg, she had been the only girl in this family. Not only did Kari gain a sister, but she felt as if she'd lost her best friend and her brother all at once.

Over the next seven years, conflict, tension, and resentment became commonplace. Sadly, the real issues between Kari and me never seemed to get addressed. We tried to put Band-Aids on our friendship—which worked fine. However, I soon learned what the acronym "fine" really stands for—*feelings inside not expressed!* And that summed it up for both of us. Kari often felt displaced, and I was constantly confused, not knowing how to interpret what was really going on. Often, this led to the silent treatment and one of us withdrawing. Since both of us hate disharmony, though, one of us would inevitably pursue the other.

Actually, we still loved each other deeply but didn't know how to communicate it. We didn't know how to manage our own feelings or deal with the underlying issues, which left us disconnected and in disharmony. The biggest hurt, however, was not just losing our dream of being family, but ultimately losing our close, intimate friendship.

One afternoon as I was home typing a paper for my master's degree program, I heard an unexpected knock at my door. I finished typing my sentence and cautiously opened the front door to see who the surprise visitor was. Wow! It was the last person I expected.

Kari stood on the front porch with tears flowing down her face. She looked broken. I reached out and embraced my sister the way I had wanted to for years. I had missed my friend so much and had wanted to comfort her in the midst of her pain, but I seemed to have been the one causing much of her discomfort.

I slowly guided Kari into my living room and sat her on the couch in front of the fireplace. I was both concerned and curious as to why she had come. I was uncomfortable, yet excited that she would open up to me again.

We engaged in small talk for just a minute until it seemed as if Kari was going to burst at the seams.

"I have something to say to you," Kari said through her tears.

I held my breath. In the past, conversations that began this way did not go well. However, this time something seemed different.

"I am so deeply sorry for all the pain we have experienced in our relationship over the years," Kari said, crying. "I don't want to go back and relive all the details, but I do want you to know how much I have missed my best friend over the years."

I stared in disbelief. I had so longed to hear these words from her.

"I want to give you something," Kari said as she handed me a small box.

It was beautifully wrapped in silver foil. Hanging from the gold ribbon was a card. I opened it slowly and cautiously.

Erin,
You are my closest friend and now my sister. I want to give you this gift as a reminder to both of us. A reminder of the love we share and the commitment we have to one another not only as friends, but as family.

As tears streamed down both of our cheeks, I unwrapped the paper and removed a small green box. Opening the hinged lid, I pulled out a beautiful, tiny bracelet. It was sterling silver and made with a continuous string of hearts. Kari took the bracelet and placed it on my left wrist.

"Erin, this is a symbol of our friendship—a friendship that will never be broken and that will never end," she said. "You are my sister and I love you. I want this bracelet to serve as a reminder of the commitment that we share to walk through the good and bad times together. I feel stupid admitting this to you, but I bought this bracelet a long time ago and never gave it to you."

Can you imagine?

I embraced my sister—my friend—and we talked and cried for hours. It was the best talk we'd had in seven years. We both took responsibility for our actions and sought forgiveness. In the end, God performed a miracle in our relationship. He used a tiny silver bracelet to restore a friendship. Our relationship is not perfect, but it is definitely much richer. It still has both peaks and valleys, but the peaks—the good times—outweigh the challenges.

Only a short time after receiving my friendship bracelet from Kari, I was able to give back to her. Kari called, weeping, and I quickly found out that she had lost her second son to a premature birth. Together, we cried and grieved the loss of baby Roger's life. A year later, Kari rushed me to the hospital when I began spotting during my third pregnancy. She sat by my bedside as an ultrasound was performed. Kari was the first to identify that we were going to be blessed with a son.

It's amazing how our friendship has come full circle! We are raising our precious children and sharing life *together*—as sisters and as friends.

Today those two bracelets—the one from Kari and the one I never gave to Jenny—are much more than pieces of jewelry to me. They are symbols of a childish friendship and a grown-up friendship, and there is a big difference between the two. The first was characterized by fun times often marred by insecurity; the second by deep joy and connection forged despite honest disagreements and unintended hurt. One represents a season of great disappointment, when I often felt rejected and displaced. The other represents new beginnings and a commitment of love, acceptance, and forgiveness.

To this day, my heart bracelet almost never leaves my wrist. It's a constant reminder of what God has in store for us through relationships—especially female friendships.

More than anything else, my coauthor, Carrie, and I desire that this book will show you just how important our friendships with women are to God. There are many books out there about female friendships; however, this book is different because it focuses on what God has taught both of us about developing grown-up friendships, such as the one I now enjoy with my sister-in-law. He has a purpose in all of our relationships, including the difficulties we encounter, and we can turn to Him for insight into our fears and reactions in the midst of challenges. Ultimately, we hope that this book will enable you to unwrap the "true gift" that God has for each of us through our female friendships.

WHY DO WE NEED FRIENDS ANYWAY?

Ever wonder why we have such a deep desire to connect with other women? I have. In fact, I have become even more curious as I have watched my daughters experience their first ups and downs with friends. My interest was especially piqued the first time my older daughter, Taylor, was wounded by a friend.

It happened several years ago, on a sunny, warm spring day in the Ozarks. I was standing, as I did every afternoon at 3:45, in a grass-covered field on the corner of North 15th Avenue.

My son, Garrison, made excited cooing noises as he saw the big yellow school bus come to a halt. He knew his sister Taylor and her friend Shelby would be scooting off soon. The bus sputtered up to the curb, and the screeching doors flew open. As Taylor trudged off the bus, I contemplated the look I saw in her eyes. Deep in my heart I recognized it. Hadn't I seen that look somewhere before? I began to panic, thinking, *Surely, it can't be—not yet! She is only seven years old.*

Soon the tears were flowing freely from my blond, pigtailed daughter. I was not quite certain what to do. How in the world could I possibly help Taylor when it was difficult for me to know how to help myself when I was hurting? I grabbed Taylor and wrapped my arms around her. I got down on my knees, looked deep into her hazel eyes, and asked her to tell me what had happened.

"Shelby doesn't want to be my friend anymore!" There it was! I knew I had recognized her look. Taylor had now been initiated into the world of pain that began back in the days of Adam and Eve.

Just three short weeks earlier, Taylor had come home from school announcing the arrival of her "new best friend—Shelby." Shelby had just transferred to her school, and as Taylor had been taught to do, she quickly befriended the new student. We discovered that Shelby lived right down the street from us, so the girls became fast and furious friends, spending as much after-school playtime together as they could.

Each morning the two girls ran to the bus stop, greeting each other with an embrace. They then jumped onto the bus and squeezed close together in one of the green vinyl bus seats (the ones that make you freeze in the cold months and sweat in the heat). They discussed their wardrobe, their homework, and their latest crushes—Billy Bob, Bubba, or Jimmy Joe (remember, we lived in the Ozark Mountains!). After school, when I met the bus, they'd typically ask if they could meet at the park again in fifteen minutes.

Then came that day when Taylor slumped off the bus alone. Thinking she might have misunderstood the situation, I tried to console her. Shaking her head, Taylor handed me a note from Shelby. In short, it said:

Taylor,
I don't want to be your friend anymore!
You don't talk to me as much as you
talk to Megan. Best friends talk to
each other more, you know . . . so if you
want to be my friend your going to have
to prove it!
Shelby

So there it was. My little girl was experiencing the pain that I've felt, not only as a young girl, but as a thirtysomething-year-old woman. I wanted to assure her that this would be the last time that she would ever feel such sharp pain and rejection, but I knew that wasn't true.

Fortunately, Taylor and Shelby soon mended their relationship. My daughter's pain diminished, and she continued to desire to make and keep friends. And five years later, both Taylor and her sister, Maddy, are experiencing the highs and lows of friendship. Meanwhile, I've been exploring the roots of our need for friendship.

CREATED FOR CONNECTION

If relationships bring such deep pain, why do we women long for them so intensely and hurt so much when they disappoint us?

The first place I looked for answers was the Bible. I noted that God recognized our need for relationship early on, when shortly after creating Adam, He said, "It is not good for the man to be alone. I will make a helper suitable for him" (Genesis 2:18). Even though Adam was close with his Creator,

God desired to give him something more—a female companion. And so God created Eve. It was a perfect relationship . . . until the deceiver entered the picture and convinced them to go against what the Lord had instructed them to do. Satan slithered into their lives and corrupted what God had intended for good.

Of course, Satan's meddling resulted in the first squabble between friends. After God found Adam and Eve hiding and ashamed, He asked them what had happened. Adam pointed his finger at Eve. Like any woman would do, Eve then blamed the source of her temptation . . . the serpent. Neither party was willing to accept responsibility for his or her actions. It's easy to come down hard on Adam and Eve, but if we look at our own track records, we have to admit that our relationships aren't in much better condition.

Aside from showing us where our friendship troubles began, the book of Genesis tells us that Adam and Eve were created *differently* for relationship. Adam tended the Garden (see Genesis 2:15), he named the animals (see Genesis 2:19), and he tilled the ground (see Genesis 3:23). He was the protector and provider of all that the Lord had granted him . . . including Eve.

Eve's role in Genesis was very different. Eve is described as the companion and child bearer. In Genesis 3:16, God said, "You will bring forth children; yet your desire will be for your husband" (NASB). Notice that God explained Adam's role in terms of his work but described Eve's in terms of her relationships.

Although Adam and Eve's story points out some of the pitfalls of relationship, Scripture offers us a look at some precious female friendships as well. Think about how Ruth followed Naomi to a foreign country, leaving her family and giving up all she ever knew. Ruth clung to her mother-in-law after Naomi had told her to leave not just once—but four times! Ruth then followed Naomi's precise instructions and was blessed through each response. The legacy Naomi leaves through Ruth is amazing—Ruth is later referred to in Scripture as a "virtuous woman" and is recognized for her strong character (see Ruth 3:11, NKJV).

What about Elizabeth and Mary? I always have found it fascinating that just a few days after finding out she was carrying the Messiah, Mary went to Elizabeth's home and stayed with her for about three months (see Luke 1:39-56). Elizabeth must have offered Mary so much wisdom and joy. In many ways Elizabeth was a mentor to Mary, as she had been down her own path of difficulties . . . especially the heartbreak of infertility. Think about how much faith and reassurance Elizabeth could offer Mary when she found herself in an unexpected situation. Elizabeth was used in Mary's life in a great way!

My search of Scripture made clear that while both men and women are made in God's relational image, women *crave* relationships innately and are driven to be in relationships in a way most men do not fully understand. Just as the Lord desires to be in relationship with us, we desire deep relationships with others.

CONFIRMATION FROM SCIENCE

As a nurse, I knew there had to be some physiological reasons for our need for intimate friendships as well. Shortly after my search to understand the girlfriend phenomenon began, I came across an intriguing research article that offers further insight into why women desire female friendships.[1] In this UCLA study, two female researchers, Shelley Taylor and Laura Klein, noted vast differences in the behavior of the male and female scientists during high-stress times in the laboratory. What they noted was that during these stressful times, the males seemed to *isolate* from others, while the females *congregated* together.

Intrigued, Drs. Klein and Taylor began pulling together information from animal research and studies examining the interaction of hormones and the nervous system. They reported that when the hormone oxytocin is released as part of the stress response in a woman, it buffers the fight-or-flight response and encourages her to tend to children and gather with other women. When she engages in this tending or befriending, studies suggest that more oxytocin is released, which further counters stress and produces a calming effect. While both men and women secrete oxytocin, estrogen enhances its effect. This calming response does not occur in men, says Dr. Klein, because testosterone—which men produce in high levels when they're under stress—seems to reduce the effects of oxytocin.

In their findings, Klein and Taylor also cite a Nurses' Health Study from Harvard Medical School that reported that the more friends women had, the less likely they were to develop physical impairments as they aged and the more likely they were to be leading a joyful life. In fact, the results were so significant that the researchers concluded that not having close friends or confidants was as detrimental to a woman's health as smoking or carrying extra weight.

This has led researchers across the country to suspect that when women hang out with their friends, they actually counteract stress. No wonder women's groups such as Mothers of Preschoolers (MOPS) and the Red Hat Society are growing in record numbers!

Since friendships serve as a buffer against stress, it's not too surprising that they promote good physical health. In her book *Friendshifts*, Jan Yager reports that having healthy female friendships can lead to:

- a longer, higher-quality life
- better odds of surviving serious medical events, such as heart attacks
- less chance of developing a respiratory infection or cancer
- less chance of experiencing depression[2]

My study of the Bible and research reports confirmed that my own desire for friendship was a part of my God-given design. Friendship is a means God uses to fulfill His good purposes in our lives . . . both through the heartwarming and the heartbreaking experiences. He uses these relationships to provide support in times of need and to bring us to our knees so we can better see our need for *Him*.[3]

Because friends provide a lifeline to women, we naturally desire these relationships. Yet many of us who long for friendships wonder why they seem so elusive. The truth is, friends don't typically knock themselves over rushing to our door. Building relationships takes time—and a willingness to risk. Because time is in short supply and risk is not at the top of most of our wish lists, we often overlook opportunities to connect with other women.

While most of this book focuses on building "grown-up" friendships—those that draw us and others closer to Christ—you can't experience those types of relationships unless you're building bonds with other women. Let's take a few moments, therefore, to consider what you can do to begin building relationships with other women, even if you've found it difficult to do so in the past.

BACK TO BASICS: BUILDING FRIENDSHIPS

We believe that, for most women, four factors are the principal barriers to building new friendships: life transitions, personality issues, personal comfort zones, and busyness.

Let's take a look at each, along with some ideas on how to overcome them.

Life Transitions

Challenge

In the past ten years, how many of these changes have you experienced: finishing school, marrying, having children, moving to a new town, going back to work, being promoted, or leaving the workforce? Any one of these can leave you with little energy or time for friends. Yet it is at exactly these times that you typically need new friends most.

Solutions

1. Look for others in the same place you are. If you meet someone going through the same type of change—or if she has dealt with it in the past—have the courage to invite her over for a cup of coffee. Don't miss the opportunity to talk with someone who might understand what you're going through. You never know what will come of the simplest interactions—in the most unexpected places.

   I know two women who became great friends because they were standing side by side in a grocery store and noticed they both had children from China. They struck up a conversation and made plans to get their daughters together later in the week. And that was that—it was the beginning of a dear friendship.

2. Join a group or start one. Many groups of women with a shared interest or experience meet regularly across the country. MOPS (Mothers of Preschoolers) was always helpful when I moved to a new community because the women attending were in the same season of life as I was. I would scan the crowd and listen—trying to identify one woman I thought I might connect with. Then I would

invite her to do something—such as have lunch together after our meeting.

Many communities have a Bible study group called "After the Boxes Are Unpacked" for women who have just moved. They come from all walks of life but have the common ground of being in an unfamiliar place. If you have gone through a divorce, churches often offer divorce recovery groups. If you are single, try the singles group at your church. You might be thinking, *No way! I am not going to* that *group!* We want to encourage you to at least try it—with an open mind. An open mind is one that is open to conversation, open to listening to others' experiences, and open to sharing what you are comfortable sharing.

Personality

Challenge

Ever met someone with a natural ability to connect with others? She has so many friends you wish she would let a few come your way! Perhaps her personality makes it easy for her to establish friendships. Maybe her family taught her the art of reaching out to others.

Making friends may not come as easily for you. It's not just a matter of whether you're naturally outgoing or shy either. Both types of women have the ability to form close friendships, and both may have difficulty making friends at times. Sometimes an outgoing person talks too much or too freely, making others uncomfortable. A quiet person may hold too much of herself in, never letting anyone too close. Either may be a terrible listener or may run from conflict and intimacy, using a ministry, job, or family obligations to hide from others.

Even if your personality makes it relatively easy for you to meet new friends, don't overlook those whose personalities seem very different from yours. The truth is, you don't have to connect only with those who share your temperament. As a matter of fact, you'll often be drawn to someone who is your complete opposite. (We'll look more closely at personality differences in chapter 6.)

Solutions

If making friends is difficult for you because of the way you are wired, consider these helpful hints:

1. If you are uncomfortable in large groups, attend functions with fewer attendees or that break into smaller groups (such as Bible studies).
2. If you have a hard time meeting people, allow others to introduce you to their friends.
3. Keep an open mind and an open stance to making friends. Let others know that you are feeling a bit isolated and looking for new companions.
4. Become really great at asking people questions about themselves. This lets them know that you are truly interested in their lives—not just your own well-being.

Comfort Zone

Challenge

Oh, how we love our comfort zones. *Merriam-Webster* defines a comfort zone as "the level at which one functions with ease and familiarity."[4] We gravitate to the familiar because we know it, it feels normal, it is easy, and it feels just right.

Our comfort zones may keep us from forming friendships with people in different life stages. If we're single, we sometimes feel uncomfortable hanging around married women. If we are married, we tend to hang out with other women who are married. When we have kids, we begin to make friends with women who have kids too—especially kids our children's ages.

You've probably heard that God works at getting us out of our comfort zones. That's not to say it's terrible to like the things in our comfort zones. I know heaven will be "just right," after all! The problem with our comfort zones here on earth is that they are narrow, limiting, and growth inhibiting. They prevent us from becoming more like Christ and discovering some of the gifts—such as unexpected friends—that He has for us when we risk being uncomfortable.

Solutions

1. Even when you're comfortable, try to keep an open door. After moving to several small towns, I understand how easy it would be to remain friends with the same gals you have known your whole life—and never make any new connections. However, as the transplanted woman in town, I can testify to how much it meant to have women reach out to me when I was new in their town. I know it blessed me, and I think about how easy it would have been for them to miss the blessings of new friends.

2. Be open to friendship with women who are different from you. I am currently in a Bible study with women from all walks of life—young and old, married and single, kids and no kids. It has allowed me to reach out and connect with women I never thought I would have anything in common with.

   One of my favorite people there is JoAnne. She is much older than I am and in a completely different season of life, but we've connected in a deep way. We became prayer partners and have prayed each other through some very challenging times. We were definitely outside of each other's comfort zones—yet all we had to do was share our hearts and hurts. The key was the willingness on both sides to reach out. Keep in mind that all women share many of the same day-to-day responsibilities—laundry, grocery shopping, making meals—whether they are single or married, working or retired. Find ways to share those tasks and do them together regardless of the season of life you are in.

Busyness

Challenge

Who can't relate to this one? Though women used to be busy together, now we are busy *and* isolated from one another. When women begin working more hours outside the home, their energy levels may decrease. By the end of the week, they may feel as if they've been sucked dry and don't really feel like reaching out to friends. Many single moms are so busy trying to hold their households together, they can't imagine finding time to make friends. I think the evil one uses the busyness of our culture to keep us isolated and alone.

Solutions

Even if your overall energy level is low, look for those times when you are not as worn down to connect with other women. That may be on the weekend or a holiday from work. Or perhaps you are an early riser and could get together before heading to your job or beginning your duties at home. Remember the need to keep balance in all areas of your life—work, home, the Lord, and yes, friendships. If one area is taking up all of your time, reevaluate your schedule. You may be shaking your head, saying, "Easy for you to say!" Yet consider the following ideas on connecting even when you're busy:

1. *Look for women who are busy with similar responsibilities.* Maybe you are working long hours during tax season. Do you know another woman who is a bookkeeper

or an accountant who would love to meet for a cup of coffee before heading home late at night? Or maybe you are a single mom who is so exhausted when you get home that you don't want to cook. Why not invite another single mom and her kids over for pizza? Always be on the lookout for others who have the same kind of schedules and duties. See if you can walk with each other through these seasons.

2. Leave room in your schedule for friends. It is so easy to make the blanket statement that "I'm just too busy." Sure, you're busy, but what are some creative ways you could make space in your schedule for friends? If you're a working mom, don't spend every lunch hour running errands or catching up on paperwork. Schedule some time for lunch with another working mom. If you're working full-time while taking classes, could you arrange to have dinner with a classmate in the student center between work and class?

3. Don't try to combat loneliness with activity rather than companionship. When you feel lonely, be careful not to fill your life with so many activities that you have no down-time to devote to friendship. Remember that connecting requires an open stance—if you always seem too busy for friends, others may get the message that you are not open to a new friendship. Leave room in your schedule for lunches, movies, or coffee with a new or an old friend!

As you take steps to initiate new friendships, trust God to help meet your friendship needs. Seasons of loneliness are not all bad, because they cause us to rely on Him even more and allow Him room to help us grow. In fact, when we invest the time and take the risks necessary to build solid friendships, we're in the perfect position to become a grown-up girlfriend.

In the next chapter, we'll explore exactly what that means.

The grown-up girlfriend . . .

. . . derives deep joy and connection, not fleeting fun marred by insecurity, from her relationships.

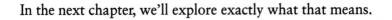

REFLECTION QUESTIONS

1. How would you describe the importance of friendships in your life? Do you feel you have the time, energy, and people skills you want to devote to your friends?

2. Can you think of a stressful time when you found yourself turning toward your girlfriends for support and encouragement? How did God use those women in that situation?

3. Do you have a memory of a childhood friendship that went sour? Can you compare and contrast it with friendship difficulties in adulthood? Do you see any similarities in things you did, said, or felt?

4. Are any of the four barriers listed on page 14 preventing you from forming meaningful friendships? If so, what is one step you could take this week to reach out to someone new?

2

WHY GOD CALLS US TO GROWN-UP FRIENDSHIPS

[Carrie and Erin]

No man is the whole of himself.
His friends are the rest of him.
GOOD LIFE ALMANAC

How to Be a Friend
Be nice and kind.
Play with them.
Let them win.
Give them a nickel.
Send them e-mails.
When they are sick, make them a card.
Ask them for a playdate.
Say great things about them.
Say it's awesome to be twins.
GIGI HANNA, AGE 7

My (Carrie's) first best friend, Trena, owned a pair of white go-go boots. Oh, how I wanted a pair! But since my mom wouldn't let me buy any, I had to settle for working my way into Trena's boots. Then I'd strut around her room, convinced I looked very cool.

My parents were best friends with hers, so it was natural that Trena and I spent many days together playing Barbies, talking, and dreaming. In the summer, we swam and water-skied at the nearby lake; every winter we watched *Rudolf, the Red-Nosed Reindeer* together at Christmastime.

Trena was the compliant, happy, and quiet one. I was the controlling, pushy, and boisterous one. Somehow it worked—she put up with my bossing her around and borrowing her treasured boots. I look back now and smile (and sometimes cringe) as I think about what kind of friend I was to Trena. I still had a lot of growing up to do when the two of us hung out together!

My next close friendship went a bit deeper. I met my friend Cindy in high school. I could talk with her about anything and always felt she accepted me just as I was. We enjoyed riding our horses together for hours. At seventeen, I had formed a friendship that looked a bit more grown up, though I still had much to learn—and still do today.

Often we begin a friendship for the same reasons I bonded with Trena and Cindy. We "like" someone. We are drawn to her. There is chemistry—common experiences and interests, fun, and laughter. What we often don't consider is whether that budding friendship has a purpose. When I think back over my friendships, I can usually see why God brought each of my friends and me together, but for most of my life I was not really seeking to understand that purpose when the friendship began. In this chapter, we'll begin by talking about the over-arching purpose that all grown-up friendships have. And what is that? To honor God by encouraging each other to become all He wants us to be. Later on in this chapter, we'll talk about how to discover the unique purpose that Christ has for each friendship.

First, you might be wondering what Erin and I mean when we talk about being a grown-up friend. This idea is based on Scripture's definition of growing up. Namely, growing up means that we develop, mature, become wiser, and take on the fruit of the Spirit and the character of Christ. It means we "put childish ways behind" (1 Corinthians 13:11) and become more mature. When the apostle Paul explained how those of us who are part of Christ's Kingdom should live, he talked about how we should relate to one another. Specifically, he urged us to be humble, gentle, patient, unified, peaceful, steadfast, and giving to one another. When we are, "we will in all things grow up into him who is the Head, that is, Christ" (Ephesians 4:15). Scripture also says that once we spoke as children, understood as children, and thought as children, but when we become adults we must put away childish things (see 1 Corinthians 13:11).

A grown-up friend is someone who encourages us in our pursuit to "grow up into him"; in fact, she desires to become like Christ too. God uses grown-up friendships to complete His purposes in us. Each day He wants us to become more like Christ Himself, embodying His character. Galatians 5:22-23 provides a list of what we are to become: more loving, joyful, peaceful, patient, kind, good, faithful, gentle, and self-controlled. Just as a child or an adolescent generally doesn't display all these attributes, so the adolescent relationship will usually come up short in producing these fruits.

Our non-Christian friends, of course, may not relate to this idea of growing up in Christ. Because we seek to make Christ the center of our lives, however, we have a responsibility to love like Christ, to forgive and communicate in healthy ways, and to resolve conflict with our friends, whether Christian or non-Christian. In many ways our witness increases in power the more "grown up" in Christ we are!

If we want to become a grown-up friend, we must embrace two premises. First, we must take seriously the goal of becoming mature and wiser. Second, we must realize that we can learn to recognize other women with this same goal and then nurture our friendships with them.

How do we know that we are growing up into all aspects of who Jesus Christ is? We may attend Bible studies and have regular quiet times with the Lord, but how are those activities transforming us? And are those changes reflected in our relationships? When we allow ourselves to grow, we think and act differently.

Remember that science project we all did as children, in which we planted the bean seed and then watched for it to grow and push its way up through the dirt in the little Styrofoam cup? Once in a while a little bean never came up. All we had to take home was the dirt and a Styrofoam cup. Bummer!

Likewise, pushing our way through the dirt in our lives can be difficult, and many of us may choose not to do so. Yet we need to be willing to look at the dirt, push our way through it, and experience the beauty of new growth. (Don't think you have any dirt? Well, we guarantee that if you ask the Lord to help you see the dirt so that you can push through it, He will. He'll also guide you and help you get past it.)

The move several years ago from Denver, where we had lived for twelve years, to Siloam Springs, Arkansas, was quite an adjustment. I left dear, sweet friends in Denver. I became pretty independent of others in our new town, feeling that nobody could replace my old friends, so why try building new friendships? Soon, though, I felt as if God was showing me that pride was really getting in my way. I realized that I was missing out on relationships as I grieved for my known friends. For the next year the password on my computer was "Humble me." I had to type that little phrase several times a day, and God worked on me to help me push through the dirt of pride. At times I felt as if I were pushing through clay rather than soft, loose dirt. As I began to focus on other people, their needs, and their unique gifts, however, I realized that pride was becoming less of a barrier in forming new friendships.

I just celebrated my forty-seventh birthday, and I will be working out these kinds of issues until I see Jesus in heaven. What keeps me going and motivated is seeing what Christ can do to cultivate intimacy and safety in my relationships. I have agreed with Him that my growth will be lifelong, but it is worth it. Can you identify the obstacles, such as shyness, pride, or busyness, that may be preventing you from enjoying all that God designed for you to experience in your relationships? Can you identify what keeps you more childish rather than mature?

As I mentioned, the second premise about grown-up friendships is that it's possible to learn how to choose grown-up friends—other women who share our goal of becoming more Christlike. Growing up is a hard task that takes focus and intimacy with Christ and His Word. We may be committed to growing up, but not everyone is invested in that goal. God does not ask us to judge people, but He does ask us to be wise and discerning. That doesn't mean we dump those friends who don't share our desire to grow up in Christ. It does mean that we may invest more time in building and nurturing grown-up friendships.

Most of us have friends who do not know Christ. In fact, some very healthy people (at least emotionally) don't know Christ as their Savior. They may communicate well, do conflict well, be sensitive to our needs, and behave with gentleness and kindness—all traits that look like Christ. Yet you'll never be able to share one key to a grown-up friendship with a non-Christian friend: prayer. As I walk through this cancer, I can't imagine not being able to call my friend and ask her to pray out loud over the phone with me in my fear or weakness.

If you don't have many friendships with fellow believers, ask God to provide Christian sisters who can fill that void and help you grow into all that Christ desires you to be. Because we desire to grow into the character of Christ, when choosing grown-up friends, we look for women who have that same desire for themselves.

The grown-up friendship is characterized by deep trust, which enables each friend to see into the heart of the other person, have empathy, and see the world from her eyes. It also enables friends to speak the truth and be honest with one another.

The more trustworthy you are, the more you will be wise about who can be trusted. That's not to say your relationships will be free of disagreements. Speaking the truth implies a willingness to go through conflict, understand differences, and even forgive one another.

Also, just because someone you've met is likable does not necessarily mean that you'll experience this level of deep understanding with her. When it does happen, though, you have attained something quite precious. When a woman desires to grow up into the image of Christ, one of the ways she can measure her progress is to see what is reflected in her friendships. After all, God uses people in our lives to sharpen us and further His refining process in us. Friendships are about fun and laughter and endearment. Yet the richest friendships go deeper than these experiences to deep trust, intimacy, and safety. Inevitably they produce growth on both sides and are characterized by a sense of purpose.

I met my friend Miss Nadine Means as a direct result of my cancer experience. She is a fellow cancer battler. We met through some friends of mine whose son is married to Nadine's daughter. While on a trip to California I met this dear woman for coffee. Ever since, we have e-mailed one another, sharing our battles and encouraging one another. We offer each other prayer, encouragement, and some humor and laughter.

We know our purpose: to encourage the other to keep a positive outlook. We laugh at our funny-looking, curly, thin chemo hair—and we laugh at our fuzzy chemo brains! We also motivate each other to support others. I have a Web site in which I journal, sharing the Word of God and reflecting on my journey with cancer. Nadine makes comfort bags for other cancer battlers.

Though we are not "best friends," we are honest, empathetic, and aware of what we bring to each other's heart. Our friendship is intentional, it's grown-up, it has purpose, and we feel touched by God.

Will you be invested in grown-up friendships? Will you be the little bean that with God's help can push through the dirt that prevents you from being all that God has called you to be within relationships? Our passion, as we write this book, is to help you do just that.

UNDERSTANDING THE PURPOSE IN YOUR FRIENDSHIP

> *Pray with your friend and speak of God together. The most profound experience in friendship is to share your encounters with Mystery.* FRIENDSHIP THERAPY[1]

While visiting a church with my family on a recent Sunday, I (Erin) was thrilled to learn from the pastor that Starbucks has quoted Rick Warren on one of their cups. Each of their coffee cups includes a quote from one of over one hundred people— some prominent, some not. Each is designed to support "good discussion." The Way I See It #92 comes from Rick Warren and says in part:

> *Focusing on yourself will never reveal your real purpose. You were made by God and for God, and until you understand that, life will never make sense. Only in God do we discover our origin, our identity, our meaning, our purpose, our significance and our destiny.*[2]

The pastor of the church we were visiting is an avid Starbucks fan. He was so excited when he found out that the coffee chain was quoting from a Christian book that he stormed into a brand-new Target and made a beeline for the Starbucks coffee shop. He rummaged through the stack of empty cups, searching for one with Warren's quote. In the meantime, the woman working the counter called security, as she was a bit taken aback to see a customer frantically sorting through the cups.

As Rick Warren points out, finding our purpose—in any area of life—means getting the focus off ourselves and what makes us feel good. Instead, we must recognize that we were "made by God and for God." We can actually allow our friends to experience Jesus through us, or we may experience Him through our friends. We need to be looking for His purpose in each friendship we have—whether it is a deep or casual one. Each gives us an opportunity to impact another's life.

When this purpose—the reason God brought you and your friend together—is recognized by both of you, it does several things:

- It takes the focus off of you and allows you to discover what God is doing. It's not about you!
- It can reduce feelings of rejection within the friendship.
- It can bring meaning and hope to the relationship—especially when the difficult and hard times come.

Let's take a closer look at these benefits.

IT TAKES THE FOCUS OFF OF YOU

I am sure you are wondering, *What is the big deal about recognizing the purpose of a relationship? Why is that so "grown-up"?* We love what Rick Warren has to say about this: "Focusing on yourself will never reveal your real purpose."

Nor will it reveal what God desires to accomplish through the friendship.

When you are focusing on Christ and not on yourself, you begin to seek Him and ask Him what He wants. We usually enter into friendships haphazardly, thinking that it is just by coincidence that we have connected with someone. Carrie and I would like to challenge that line of thinking. Over and over again, we have discovered that when we are willing and watching for the purpose to be revealed, we will get the glorious opportunity of seeing how God is using that friendship. Remember, He promises us in 2 Corinthians 1:4 that He "comforts us in all our troubles, so that we can comfort those in any trouble." This is exactly what we are talking about. In accomplishing His plan for our lives, God will orchestrate and align us with others who have had experiences that they can share with us or experiences we can share—in order to mold us and others into a brighter image of Him. You are not an accident—nor are the friends you cross paths with. As the Bible tells us, "In his heart a man plans his course, but the LORD determines his steps" (Proverbs 16:9).

I (Erin) truly believe that one reason my family moved to Siloam Springs this past year was because the Lord knew what Carrie and her family were going to experience. In January 2005, we had agreed to come to John Brown University so that my husband, Greg, could work with Carrie and Gary Oliver at the university's Center for Relationship Enrichment. Greg and I both felt the Lord leading us there. Since we were happy in our community and work in Missouri, we did not understand His leading, but we both knew in our hearts (after many nights of tears and prayer) that it was the right thing. Carrie was struggling with her health at that point, and in May, she was diagnosed with cancer. As we grieved over the devastating news, we suddenly realized that this may have been part of why the Lord wanted us to be in Siloam Springs—to encourage the Olivers in the midst of a great trial.

Because Carrie and her husband, Gary, had been such great mentors to Greg and me when we were newlyweds, we had often asked the Lord, "What could we ever do to repay them for what they have done for us?" You see, we had lived in Denver near Carrie and Gary during our very tumultuous first year of marriage. They were further down the road and trained in helping distressed couples, and we definitely met that criterion. Our marriage would not be the same today if not for their encouragement and guidance in the midst of some trying times. Now it's our turn to encourage the Olivers.

Ultimately, instead of being haphazard and unaware of the purpose of our relationships, we are encouraging you to pray and ask the Lord for His purpose in each friendship you become involved in. And then be ready to embrace that purpose rather than ignore what He is calling you to do.

Keep an open mind about this. In the midst of your interactions with others, be on the lookout for what God's purpose might be. We can best do this not only by listening to the Lord after seeking Him, but also by listening to our friend. Become great at asking questions and seeking more information about this person and her situation. As you learn about her, the Lord may reveal more to you.

Now, I can imagine you might be thinking, *Not all my interactions will be long-drawn-out conversations with great purposes.* I agree with you; however, when talking with a friend, you never know how your presence right then is being used to bring comfort, encouragement, or companionship to someone who might be lonely, hurting, or confused. The Lord knows, however, and we have the opportunity to adopt the attitude that there might be a greater purpose than we can see in any interaction.

It's Not about You!

If we truly recognize that the Lord is in control of whom we cross paths with, it becomes easier to see that our relationships are really about *Him* and not *us*! We have to admit that when we enter into a new relationship, we often do so because it feels good or it meets a need for us. We feel loved, valued, and worthwhile. The relationship may fill gaps in our lives. I'm not aware of many women who enter into friendships excitedly because the other woman hurt their feelings, blew up at them, or passed on a piece of gossip. There is always the opportunity to work through trials and become friends; however, ultimately we enter a relationship because the initial connection feels good. Much like dating, we put our best foot forward and are on our best behavior.

However, where does it go from there? What is the next step in our relationship? Will we continue in a friendship simply because it meets our needs, or are we willing to truly seek how the Lord might be leading us to higher ground or using us to encourage our friend to higher places?

Obviously, just because a new friendship feels good does not make it a bad thing, but if we are not intentional about discovering the deeper purpose of our friendship, we end up setting ourselves up for pain, feelings of rejection, and disappointment.

It Reduces Feelings of Rejection

Reduce feelings of rejection? We'll sign up for that! No one likes to be hurt, though at some point we all experience the sting of rejection. However, if we truly embrace God's plan and take ownership of the real purpose in a relationship, we take responsibility for our own emotional health and well-being rather than relying on our friend to provide it. When we truly recognize that one of the purposes in a relationship is to glorify Christ, the friendship becomes about Him rather than us. It leads us to have focus and direction—a "goal" in the friendship.

When we have focus, we are in the friendship for a reason: Perhaps we are encouraging each other in the workplace or praying together for our children or challenging one another to better health (physically as well as spiritually) or consciously allowing God to use the strength or experience of someone else to foster growth in us. Focusing in this way really makes the relationship fun!

One fond memory I (Erin) have is of the day I received a phone call from a casual friend named Tammy. Tammy had no idea what was going on in my life; however, she happened to call during a trying time. Tammy said, "I heard that you enjoy working out, and I am looking for someone to exercise with me. I wanted to call and ask you—would you be interested in working out together?"

After silently celebrating by jumping up and down in my kitchen, I immediately responded, "Yes! You have no idea how much I could use this!" Because I'm an extrovert, working out with someone else is always more fun than being alone, and in the midst of lots of stress, I had also gained several extra pounds. About a week later, Tammy began showing up at my house around 6:30 a.m. on Monday, Wednesday, and Friday. We would alternate working out with weights and running on the treadmill.

There were days that I never would have stepped near anything that possibly would have made me sweat, but because Tammy was there, I did it. Sometimes we discussed difficulties within parenting or our marriages. We would then pray and encourage each other in the midst of our emotional stress, while we were alleviating stress in a physical manner as well.

Tammy had no idea how much I needed her in my life during that season, but because she was willing to listen to the Lord's leading, she truly blessed me. I am certain it ended up being a mutual blessing. Although our original purpose was working out to become physically fit, we ended up accomplishing two goals at once. We became more fit, but we also encouraged each other during challenging times.

It is little prompts such as these from the Lord that we need in order to become better at hearing so we can respond to His call and His focus! He may have you lined up not only to bless someone else but also to receive great blessing in return. It we refuse to listen, we may not only miss out on being used in our friend's life but also miss out on His best for our lives.

IT BRINGS MEANING AND HOPE

Just because you recognize the purpose of a grown-up friendship doesn't mean you'll never experience any stress or tension in that relationship. It does mean, however, that you *can* find meaning and hope.

This is especially important when we are searching for what God wants to do when the hurts come. Hope can carry us through the most difficult of times. The hurt may be due to the relationship itself or a trial we are experiencing. Expect the challenges. It is not a matter of *if* but *when* the hurts come. When we are seeking Him and have His purpose in mind, the challenging times can be viewed with meaning. It may be that He is teaching us about becoming less critical and more accepting of our friend, or maybe He is calling us to speak truth to our friend about an area in her life that is dark. Constantly seeking Him within our friendships, both in the hard times and the good times, will ultimately lead us to Him. He will reveal to us His meaning and purpose, and He will bathe us with His hope.

In the next chapter, we will discuss asking God for wisdom in determining the level of intimacy He desires for each friendship.

The grown-up girlfriend...

... honors God by encouraging her friend to become all He wants her to be.

. . . .

REFLECTION QUESTIONS

1. Can you describe a friendship you've had that wasn't very grown up? What part did you play in preventing that relationship from becoming more mature? What part did your friend play?

2. What may be preventing you from pushing through the dirt to become more grown up and more like Christ?

3. How do you typically choose your friends? Do you do so intentionally or haphazardly?

4. Why is it important to be able to establish a grown-up friendship?

5. Is discovering the purpose in your friendships a new concept for you? Are you aware of the purpose of each of the close friendships in your life right now? If so, identify what those purposes are.

6. What point in this chapter might God use to improve your closest friendships?

3

ᴛHE GROWN-UP FRIEND
EXPERIENCES LEVELS OF INTIMACY

[Erin]

*We can never replace a friend. When a man is
fortunate enough to have several, he finds they are
all different. No one has a double in friendship.*
FRIEDRICH VON SCHILLER

*Let your friendship be large or small, tall or short,
square or round, paisley or plain. Friendships come
in every size and shape and shade imaginable.*
FRIENDSHIP THERAPY

Shortly after having my third child, Garrison, I began struggling to manage the demands of my family, my home, my marriage, my commitments at church, and last but not least, my
friends. My world seemed overwhelming. I clearly remember
one day when I was preparing dinner as my girls were charging
through the house and my newborn was nursing frantically.
Suddenly the phone began to ring.

I remember thinking, *I am a multitasking type of girl—I can
do this.* I answered the phone and was greeted by my girlfriend
Nancy, whom I so longed to reconnect with. I sat down to continue nursing the baby and launched into a "girl" conversation.
A few minutes later, the timer on my oven began ringing. *Oh
yeah,* I thought, *I was making dinner too.* Silently assessing the

situation, I decided I might be able to manipulate the phone cord into the kitchen. I figured if I pulled extra hard to make it to the oven while nursing the baby, I could do everything at once. However, when I began to pull the hot cookie sheet out, nearly bruising my precious son's head, the phone cord suddenly gave way, and the phone receiver flew off my shoulder and into the other room. After running to pick it up, I began to apologize to Nancy, only to hear her laughing exuberantly on the other end. We were too much alike: She knew exactly what I had been trying to accomplish and that I had failed. At that moment I wondered, *Lord, how can I do it all?* I felt torn in a million directions when all I had really wanted was a five-minute conversation!

After this experience, I began to discuss my dilemma with others. Soon I discovered that I was not the only woman who felt pulled in so many different directions while still needing to find time to connect with other women.

One conversation changed my life forever. I was sitting on the front porch of my in-laws' home. My mother-in-law, Norma, could tell I was struggling, trying to keep it together. At her prompting, I explained how I was feeling—overloaded, yet grieving because I was not able to keep up with friends. She knew I tended to be extroverted and that I was energized when I was around others, especially my friends.

Norma gave me the perfect word picture that day. She said, "Erin, friends are actually like baskets." This perplexed me. *My friends are like what? Baskets?* As she explained what the baskets represented, I realized that I had been attempting to make all my friendships deep and intimate—in essence, all the same level of deep intimacy. And in that season of my life— mothering young kids—I quickly realized why my friendships had become so challenging to keep up with.

ASSESS YOUR SITUATION

At about the same time as my talk with my mother-in-law, I came across this verse: "A man of many companions may come to ruin" (Proverbs 18:24). I realized quickly that I could apply it to my situation. Can you relate to it as well? Have you ever run yourself ragged trying to please and meet the needs of every friend you have? When we do, we either become out-of-balance people or frazzled friends, or we relegate ourselves to carrying on surface friendships with no real quality or depth. Here I think Solomon was reminding us that the depth of a person's friendships is more important than the number of friends he or she has. At the same time, trying to meet every friend's needs will drain us.

Extroverts, those energized by their contact with others, are more likely to wear themselves out. Introverts, those who recharge by spending time alone, are more likely to exist on surface relationships. In her book *If You Ever Needed Friends, It's Now*, Leslie Parrott reports that the average person comes in contact with between 500 and 2,500 people in one year, largely depending on whether she is extroverted or introverted.[1] Introverted women generally meet a smaller number of people, while extroverted women usually come in contact with more people. Just think how unrealistic it would be to think that we could become friends with all 2,500 of these individuals—500 would be difficult for most of us!

WHAT ARE THE SEVEN LEVELS OF INTIMACY?

Before explaining that life-transforming truth about the baskets of friendship, it would help to acknowledge that we communicate at different levels of intimacy with everyone we meet each day—whether our spouse, our closest friend, or the clerk at the dry cleaner. Matthew Kelley summarizes these levels in his book *The Seven Levels of Intimacy*.[2]

- Level one: We share clichés.
- Level two: We share facts.
- Level three: We share opinions.
- Level four: We share hopes and dreams.
- Level five: We share feelings.
- Level six: We share faults, fears, and failures.
- Level seven: We share our legitimate needs.

Kelley explains that no relationship is confined to any single level of communication. He also points out that the levels of intimacy are not a task to be carried out with the intention of working up through the levels: "Oh . . . we reached level four today . . . let's go to five tomorrow." Last, but so important, he explains that not all relationships will experience all seven levels of intimacy, nor are they meant to. Some relationships belong in the first level of intimacy only!

Okay, Okay—Where Do the Baskets Come In?

This is what I realized when talking with my mother-in-law that spring day. I came to understand that there are different levels of intimacy in my life and that relationships within the different levels have different purposes, different expectations, and different boundaries.

The basket system can help you evaluate all the friendships in your life. There are three baskets: basket number three, basket number two, and basket number one. Now please understand that this is not meant to be a hard-and-fast rule-oriented model. It provides a broad perspective to get you thinking about the women God has placed in your life and what He intends for each relationship. As you read through the description of each level of friendship, begin to think through the following questions:

- Which basket does each of my friends fall into?
- Are my baskets empty or too full?
- Am I experiencing true intimacy in my closest friendships? Why or why not?

I realize that in applying the symbolism of baskets, you may feel uncomfortable, sensing that it feels too categorizing or exclusive. You may even begin to feel insecure, wondering which basket your friends would place you in. When speaking about the basket analogy to groups of women, I hear the same question over and over again: "If you have someone in your number one basket, does it matter if you are in theirs?"

It's possible that some of your friends might put you into a different basket than you would place them in. I actually don't think that matters; you and your friends each have your own basket. Each of you must decide for yourself whom you consider to be your most intimate friends. So someone you consider a basket one friend may love you dearly but not consider you to be as intimate of a friend. While it's nice when someone you consider a close friend thinks the same thing about you, it doesn't always have to be that way. In fact, I rarely disclose to my friends what basket I've placed them in. Often, it simply serves as a framework for me as I evaluate my relationships.

I encourage you to view this basket system only for the purpose of defining your relationships with others. I pray that you can use it as a tool to put your own relationships into proper perspective and to guide you as you seek to determine the focus of your relationships. Ultimately, my hope is that this system will help you better love the Lord, others, and yourself. We are called to love everyone, yet we are not called to share intimately with everyone.

BASKET NUMBER THREE: ACQUAINTANCES
(20 to 100 individuals)

- You know these people by name.
- You usually share facts or clichés.
- This could be a cashier at the grocery store or the secretary at your doctor's office.[3]

At one time in my life, one of my basket three friends was the waitress at a local Sonic restaurant. I frequented this fast-food restaurant so often that she had my daily order memorized. When I would drive up and push the button to place my order, Carolyn would come on and say, "I've got it coming out . . . one large Diet Coke with lime wedges." I would laugh and think, *I really have a problem!*

After several months, my husband began to question my frequent stops, saying he didn't think this could possibly fit into our budget. I began to realize that it was no longer just the Diet Coke I was after; it was the relationship with my new friend, Carolyn. I don't know that Greg bought into my explanation that I was "building a relationship"—I even threw in "for the Kingdom"—but truly that was what it was for me. Although it never went beyond my order and a quick "How are you doing today?" my daily interaction with Carolyn was a sweet basket number three relationship. (This relationship cost me $1.32 every day . . . hopefully, yours won't cost you!)

BASKET NUMBER TWO: GOOD FRIENDS OR COMPANIONS *(5 to 20 individuals)*

- You talk beyond the surface with these individuals.
- You share opinions or concerns—maybe moving to the third and fourth levels of intimacy at times.

- You typically have something in common with these gals . . . you could call them "special-interest friends."
- She could be a friend who has kids the same age as yours, a friend with whom you exercise or share a hobby (such as scrapbooking or cooking), or someone who started a new job or moved into a new community at the same time you did.
- There may be a defined purpose in this friendship or a shared activity that may or may not continue long term.

I realized how powerful the basket concept can be when I applied it to a friendship that I had been attempting to make a basket one relationship. It was a frustrating friendship at times—I often had to explain why I did what I did to this particular friend because I did things so differently than she. She was detail oriented and I wasn't. I was fun-loving and spontaneous, and she liked to schedule out her days months before they arrived. She was on the opinionated side, and I often found myself shutting down because I felt run over by her personality. However, I truly enjoyed some aspects of this relationship, so I didn't want to walk away from it. We both loved the Lord and attended the same church. Our husbands enjoyed each other's company. We could go out to lunch with friends we had in common and truly have a pleasant experience.

When I applied the basket analogy to this friendship, I realized that we could remain great friends, just not intimate friends. I no longer had unrealistic expectations about what she could provide for me—or what I could provide for her. It allowed me to put enough space into the relationship to have perspective. You know how sometimes when you are standing too close to a picture, you need to take a few steps back and get a new perspective? That was exactly what I needed to do in this friendship. Stepping back allowed me to appreciate all the good characteristics in my friend and adjust my expectations to an appropriate level. It also took away the need to change each other, because there was enough space to embrace our differences. Soon, I began to realize that this friend was a joy and a blessing as a basket number two friend. At times we share deeply, but with realistic expectations. This friendship continues to enrich me today.

BASKET NUMBER ONE: KNOW-IT-ALL FRIENDS
(1 to 4 individuals)

- You share your needs and feelings, possibly moving to the fifth, sixth, and seventh levels of intimacy at times.
- These are friends of the heart and soul.
- These friendships require more time.
- These friendships have a higher level of trust and commitment.
- You're more likely to need to walk through conflict and manage relational dynamics with these friends.

In her book *Treasured Friends*, Ann Hibbard discusses the importance of our basket number one friends.

> *Our closest circle of friends operates like a trust circle. We all go through times when crippled by pain or tragedy; we become dead weight in our relationships. We fall. Who is there to prevent us from hitting the ground? If we have a large number of acquaintances but no true friends, the circle that they form is too far away. They are not close enough to break our fall.*
>
> *On the other hand, if we have only a few very close friends, they will not be able to provide a tight circle for us. There will be gaps. And two or three people will soon grow weary.*[4]

During that season of chaos I described at the beginning of this chapter, I began asking the Lord for discernment to determine whom He had brought into my life for deep connection. He quickly answered my prayers, and I began building deeper relationships with three women who eventually became my basket number one friends. We had been friends for quite some time, but not at a really deep level.

We were each in a unique season of life. I had just had my third baby, Lisa had just had her first child after longing for one for years, Nancy was adapting to working part-time, and Janet had experienced a broken heart over another friendship. God knew that we all longed for healthy friendships that would support and encourage us during our separate trials. This allowed us to become very intentional about our friendships and really seek the Lord about His purpose for these relationships. We all had other friends, but we recognized that these friendships were designed to lead each of us to become more Christlike as we offered each other love and support and spoke the truth to one another. This became a safe haven for each of us during some challenging times.

Although two of us have since moved away, we continue to cherish our times together. We take a trip once a year, and during our last trip (the fifth one), we took time to intentionally get deep. We spent time reflecting on our year—what had happened that was great and what was most painful. We also spent time in prayer together, lifting each other up.

However, over the years, we've had to work through some misunderstandings. This is not always easy to do . . . but it is so necessary in friendships that are more intimate. Several years ago, I could feel an unspoken strain with one of these precious friends, Janet. I prayed about bringing up the situation—because for me that is always the hardest part. I couldn't decide if this tension would just go away on it own.

And honestly, I prefer to avoid conflict, so it would have been easier to wish it away. However, our annual fall trip was approaching, and I knew I didn't want anything to go unspoken before our fun girls' trip. So I waited until the night before—the last possible minute, of course—and brought it up over the phone. Though I would have preferred to have this kind of conversation in person, I realized it was my last chance—*Now or never,* I thought.

So I gently said to Janet, "I feel like there has been tension between us lately and really wanted to check this out with you. I think I know what has been going on with me, but I'd love to hear from you first." She responded by saying, "Erin, I have just felt like you have been distant with me lately for reasons I haven't been able to understand. I haven't been sure whether you want me around or not."

I immediately understood what she was saying, because it was true—I realized I had put some boundaries in place without really being aware of it. I immediately validated Janet by saying, "I definitely see how you would have been left wondering what was going on with me—because I think that I actually have been feeling like you didn't need me around lately. There have been a few times that decisions have been made without my input even though they involved me. That made me feel like I wasn't needed or necessary in the mix. So I think I then reacted by putting up some firm boundaries."

We both said we definitely did want the other around and affirmed our love for one another. We were able to go on our trip and have a blast without the tension. Boy, was I glad that I had brought it up and cleared up a relatively simple misunderstanding.

While this situation ended well, I have experienced more complicated conflicts with other friends that didn't end as well. However, I'm usually able to see what I can learn from the challenge and how God is using the discomfort in my life. Relational discomfort and disharmony lead me to grief and sadness and then to brokenness. I end up on my face in front of Him—exactly where I needed to be all along. This is when He can mold me and change me to become more like Him. As we all know, this is not always an easy process; however, I know for me it is a necessary one.

THE PLACE OF BASKETS IN THE BODY OF BELIEVERS

I was reminded not long ago of the powerful role friends play in the body of Christ. In August 2005, my husband and I left a ministry in Branson, Missouri, and moved to Siloam Springs, Arkansas. About four months after arriving in this quaint town, we learned that my mom (who lives in Phoenix) had just been diagnosed with lung cancer. Although I was supported from afar by many dear friends, I was truly overwhelmed by the support we received from the women of Siloam Springs. It brings me to tears to think about how we experienced Christ's love through these women.

My husband insisted that I travel to be with my mom in Phoenix; however, I don't think he had thought through how he was going to handle the kids' schedules and child care, all in the midst of having a brand-new job and living in a new community. I will never forget calling home and hearing Greg say, "I am overwhelmed with the amount of support and help that I have received from your friends, especially your friends from Bible study and our small group." What a precious feeling to realize that these new friends cared deeply for our family as brothers and sisters in Christ—enough to help with the kids, bring meals in the evening, and even move us from our rental house to our new home. I was blown away by what a group of women could plan and pull off with the help of their husbands. Women are resourceful . . . aren't we?

The wonderful thing about the basket system is that when you have friends at all three levels, others are there to step in and meet needs. It truly functions as a full body of believers, which is what I believe God desires our community of friends to be.

Ultimately, God used the analogy of the baskets to help me:

- Recognize that there are different levels of intimacy in my friendships. Not all my friends will emerge as basket number one friends.
- Evaluate the quality of my relationships. Am I experiencing true intimacy in any of my relationships, or am I spread too thin, trying to have too many intimate friendships?
- Identify and become intentional about finding those whom the Lord wants me to make my basket number one friends. ("A righteous man is cautious in friendship" [Proverbs 12:26].) What is God's purpose for each of these friends in my life? What is my purpose in their lives?
- Understand the need for a full community of women in my life . . . not all at the same level of intimacy, but all precious and important. This has created more balance in my friendships.
- Evaluate whether I relate to the Lord as a basket number one friend. When He is in the dead center of basket number one, His love not only can flow into my life but also is released so I am able to love all the women He has brought into my life. ("God is love" [1 John 4:16].)

I had a rude awakening when I realized that I had been attempting to replace God with human relationships. This is a common error women make. Our default setting, especially in times of difficulty, is to turn to other people or things. However, we quickly learn that human relationships can never provide what the heavenly Father can provide for us. Humans can and will fail us. And the great news is that He *never* will.

Where is God in your baskets? Has He slipped into a basket number three role, with limited intimacy shared? Where do you desire Him to be?

JESUS HAD BASKETS

We can apply the basket analogy to Jesus' relationships when He walked on earth. He valued and honored every person He came in contact with; however, He did not make every relationship a basket number one.

> **Basket Number Three:** Jesus had many acquaintances. He took every opportunity to direct each person He came in contact with to His heavenly Father.

> **Basket Number Two:** The disciples were not all intimate friends. However, they were extremely important in His life. Jesus took the time to pray and seek His Father's wisdom on who should be His disciples (see Luke 6:12-13).

> **Basket Number One:** Peter, James, and John seemed especially close to Jesus and were with Him in the garden of Gethsemane in His final hours on the earth. In the garden, Jesus revealed His need for true friends and for a core relationship with His heavenly Father. Jesus knew what lay ahead for Him—namely, death on a cross—and He needed time to prepare His heart in prayer. Jesus pleaded with Peter, James, and John to stay awake and pray. His plea revealed His full humanity and His soul's need for companionship, especially at His darkest hour.[5]

In Jesus' moment of deepest need, He withdrew a bit farther to be alone with His heavenly Father. Although He showed His need for friendships in Matthew 26:36-46, Mark 14:32-42, and Luke 22:39-46, we also see that these friendships were no substitute for His primary relationship with His heavenly Father.

I believe that Jesus modeled for us what our relationships should look like. All humans have innate value, and we are called to love each person; however, we are not called to be intimate with all of them, nor are we called to the same level of intimacy with each of them. Just as with Jesus, all our friendships are important, but each has a different purpose.

MOLDED TO GOD'S IMAGE

Shortly after moving to Siloam Springs, I developed a precious friendship with Stacey. Months into our friendship, she began to realize that my deepest love language is gifts. In other words, nothing makes me feel more loved and appreciated than receiving a gift from a friend or family member. Naturally, I also love to give gifts, and I had picked up several gifts for Stacey. Finally, she mentioned that she had a gift for me at home that she kept forgetting to give me. Of course, my heart pounded at the mention of a gift! It so speaks to my heart! Each time she came to my house, I would nonchalantly look to see if she was carrying anything extra—but time after time there was nothing.

The night finally came. She and her husband had come over, and she arrived carrying a beautifully wrapped present. Without acting too impulsively, I ripped into it and found a gorgeous handmade clay basket. My husband immediately piped up: "How sweet. You gave her a basket." He knew that I talk about the baskets frequently and assumed that Stacey must have put that all together.

Quickly, she fumbled and said, "Oh yes, it *is* a basket"—

then she admitted that she hadn't been thinking of my talks when selecting a gift for me. I then launched into a "dissertation" on my basket theory.

With that in mind, Stacey decided to send Sylvie, a close friend of hers in Houston, a basket identical to mine. She explained to Sylvie what she now understood about the basket system, adding that the two of them had definitely been basket number one friends all along; they just hadn't known what to call it! Stacey added that the Lord had used their friendship to mold both of them, much as He molded the basket from clay (see Jeremiah 18:6).

Wow! I immediately connected with this, as the Lord has in fact used so many women in my life to mold me and change me. It hasn't always felt good or ended positively, but He has used these relationships to shape me more and more into His image. Can you identify with this in your own life?

The grown-up girlfriend . . .

. . . considers God's purpose for each of her friendships, knowing not all will reach the same level of intimacy.

. . . .

REFLECTION QUESTIONS
1. How can you apply the basket concept to your friendships?

2. Do you have friends in each basket? Do you have too few or too many in any basket?

3. If there is a need in one particular basket, spend time (maybe even right now) asking the Lord to fill that need.

4. Where does the Lord fit into your baskets?

The Grown-Up Friend Is Committed to Knowing Herself

[Erin]

To be a good friend, value yourself. To treasure another's essence in your heart, you must first treasure the precious essence that is you.
Friendship Therapy

Allow yourself to be loved by your friend. When your friend knocks on the door of your heart with love, put out the welcome mat of your longing-to-be-loved self.
Friendship Therapy

I remember the first time I got to hear a heart beating through my stethoscope in nursing school. *Lub-dub, lub-dub.* The beat was regular and steady. My friend Missy laughed as we both awkwardly practiced the technique our professor was showing us to hear each other's heart rhythm. That was the first time I recognized the power of our hearts. After graduating and becoming a labor and delivery nurse, I had the joy of hearing the fetal heartbeat each time I came to work. Sometimes panic would set in if the heart rate slowed as a new life was about to enter the world. On the other hand, there was nothing more satisfying than hearing a newborn cry, since it signaled that the heart rate was at an acceptable level. Three years after beginning my nursing career, I unexpectedly had the pleasure of hearing a heart beat within *my* abdomen.

When I went home to Phoenix this past Christmas, I had no idea how difficult the trip would be. My mom was in the process of medical testing that led to a cancer diagnosis. She had been hospitalized for two days before I arrived. I remember walking into her hospital room—ironically at one of the hospitals where I had done some of my nursing training years ago—and noticing how different this unit was from the baby units I had worked on. Still, so many memories flooded back. I leaned over my mom's bedside and embraced her, and I will never forget how comforting it was to hear her heart beating. *Lub-dub, lub-dub.* Slow and regular. It was an indicator of the power that the heart brings—life.

Considering how central our physical hearts are to sustaining life, I'm not surprised that the Lord emphasizes how critical the heart is in our relationships with Him and others. And what is the heart? It is the vital center of one's being, emotions, and sensibilities.[1] The Bible includes over 955 verses about the heart. Just consider what a few of these passages tell us about the importance of our hearts to our connection with God (all italics have been added for emphasis):

- "My *heart* grew hot within me, and as I meditated, the fire burned; then I spoke with my tongue." (Psalm 39:3)
- "Above all else, guard your *heart*, for it is the wellspring of life." (Proverbs 4:23)
- "As [a man] thinketh in his *heart*, so is he." (Proverbs 23:7, KJV)
- "You will seek me and find me when you seek me with all your *heart*." (Jeremiah 29:13)
- "Blessed are the pure in *heart*, for they will see God." (Matthew 5:8)

- "Out of the overflow of the *heart* the mouth speaks." (Matthew 12:34)
- "The seed on good soil stands for those with a noble and good *heart*, who hear the word, retain it, and by persevering produce a crop." (Luke 8:15)
- "Where your treasure is, there your *heart* will be also." (Luke 12:34)
- "Now that you have purified yourselves by obeying the truth so that you have sincere love for your brothers, love one another deeply, from the *heart*." (1 Peter 1:22)[2]

Exploring my own heart was the beginning of the journey of truly knowing myself. It has been both difficult and fulfilling. If I had ignored my heart, I would have experienced emotional death; however, guarding it has brought about abundant life.

WHAT IS THE STATE OF YOUR HEART?

One of the teachers of the law came and heard them debating. Noticing that Jesus had given them a good answer, he asked him, "Of all the commandments, which is the most important?" "The most important one," answered Jesus, "is this: 'Hear, O Israel, the Lord our God, the Lord is one. Love the Lord your God with all your heart and with all your soul and with all your mind and with all your strength.' The second is this: 'Love your neighbor as yourself.' There is no commandment greater than these."

MARK 12:28-31

Throughout this book we talk about how to be a great friend to others, but central to this idea is that we must first be a great friend to ourselves. We would never encourage you to throw yourself into a basket number one friendship without taking the time to really get to know someone. Likewise, we believe that to be a great friend to yourself, you must take the time to get to know yourself and your heart. After all, the second greatest commandment is to "love your neighbor as yourself."

Have you ever been outside and noticed the sow bugs, better known as "roly-poly bugs"? They are fascinating little creatures. These little gray bugs roll up into a ball when they are touched. They actually form a ball when they sense a looming threat. And have you ever tried to get one to open once it has rolled into its safety position? It is impossible, and I suspect that if you did get it to open up, the bug would die.

This is exactly what our hearts do. When we feel threatened or hurt, our hearts are just like the sow bugs. Like them, we close off because we don't feel safe.

With that in mind, think through a hurtful experience in one of your friendships. Was your heart open or closed? Very likely, you closed off your heart to the other person as soon as you were hurt. The problem with this response is that we were created to exist with an open heart.

Paula and Beth had been great friends for about a year. Their husbands actually connected too, and they knew what a blessing that was, since it isn't easy to build a relationship between couples in which all four people connect. Paula and Beth spent their days together shopping and having lunch out, as they were both at home awaiting the births of their first babies. On the weekends, they would get together along with their husbands for dinner, usually at Paula's brand-new house. But as they both approached their sixth month of pregnancy, Paula began to notice that Beth's attitude toward her was changing.

"Everything became a competition between us—except I didn't want to compete," says Paula. "I wanted my fun, supportive friend back, but the more I hoped for that, the worse it seemed to be. Beth would criticize the meals I prepared and the things I chose to buy for my nursery, and she even compared the way our bodies looked while we were pregnant. It was bizarre!"

After a few months, Paula began reaching out to other friends because it wasn't fun to be with Beth anymore. Paula says, "Once I began to look for other support, Beth seemed to become even more critical and nasty to me. I just didn't know what else to do because I couldn't handle the way she treated me anymore. I wanted to be away from her and with friends who were uplifting. I had no need for a friend who constantly criticized me and compared everything we did or bought. It reminded me too much of my mother."

Beth delivered her baby first, and Paula had her baby about one month later. Both had boys. Paula grieves, wishing their friendship could have been saved, but she says she doesn't think she could handle Beth's attitude along with all the stress of having a newborn. She says, "The saddest thing for me is that our sons could have grown up together as friends, but now they don't even know each other, even though we live in the same town. Quite frankly, it is just a shame."

Like Paula, when we're hurt, we often put walls in place to guard our hearts because we feel emotionally unsafe. We fear that our hearts will be hurt again. Women often say, "I don't like my friend anymore, and I definitely don't feel any 'love' toward her anymore." The tragedy is that when we walk away, we may forfeit a friendship that not only could have survived the conflict but possibly even moved to a deeper level of understanding—maybe even to a basket number one friendship. However, this happens only when we don't allow our hearts to close.

Until I began considering how easy it was for me to close my heart, whenever I had an interaction with a friend that didn't feel good, I would walk away upset. Then I would become frustrated with myself for feeling the way I did and attempt to pry my heart back open so I could reengage in the relationship. That just left me feeling more unsafe—not only with my friend but with myself. When I tried to force my heart open, I was not guarding and caring for it, so there was a part of me that was left uncertain that I could do a good job of protecting my heart. Also, others saw me as indifferent or distant.

So if we shouldn't force our hearts open once they're closed, how do we keep them open? First, we shouldn't ignore that we don't feel loving toward another person; instead, we must challenge our beliefs about love and its origins. We tend to assume that we can crank up the old love generator and create love on our own. When we don't feel love toward our friend, we put enormous pressure on ourselves to make ourselves feel love. And when that doesn't happen, we decide that either we're incapable of generating love (so there must be something wrong with us) or our friend is unlovable (so there is something wrong with her), or that something is amiss with the relationship itself.

In reality, no love comes from us. We are not the originators. God is.

> *Dear friends, let us love one another, for love comes from God. Everyone who loves has been born of God and knows God. Whoever does not love does not know God, because God is love. . . . There is no fear in love. But perfect love drives out fear, because fear has to do with punishment. The one who fears is not made perfect in love. We love because he first loved us.* 1 JOHN 4:7-8, 18-19

The point is this: You and I cannot generate a single drop of love. It all comes from God. By receiving God, we receive His love. We can then open our hearts and share love with others. Loving feels good to us, but we are just passing on what we've received from God. In other words, we can make a conscious decision to receive God's love so we can pass love on to our friends—regardless of what they've done. We know our hearts are open when we experience a deep, emotional connection to another human being.

On the other hand, when a woman says she no longer feels love toward her friend, she generally has closed the door to her heart to prevent the flow of love. When one or both friends have lost heart, the friendship deteriorates. They are completely disconnected from their hearts—especially their emotions. When our hearts are closed, God's love cannot come from Him, through us, to others. And we won't feel loving toward them. If our hearts are closed, then we have shut out God's love. This is what is actually happening when people do not feel love toward their friend. No matter how justifiable the reason seems, the result is the same: We have simply closed our hearts to our friend.

People who have shut their hearts often exist in a black-and-white world, and their hearts are shut down. They don't feel. They rationalize or numb themselves to life and to the state of their hearts. They could be described as detached, indifferent, numb, lifeless, heartless, alone, emotionally unavailable, or hard-hearted.

Do you feel that way? Do others accuse you of being this way? It's like what the Tin Man (from *The Wizard of Oz*) experienced: "It was a terrible thing to undergo, but during the year I stood there I had time to think that the greatest loss I had known was the loss of my heart. While I was in love I was the happiest man on earth; but no one can love who has not a heart, and so I am resolved to ask Oz to give me one."[3]

This is the key. The issue is not how we can love our friends. Since we cannot generate love on our own, the focus needs to be changed to the state of our hearts. The real question becomes: "Is my heart open or closed to my friend?" If we realize our hearts are closed and we want to change that, we need to focus our energy on making our relationships safe through appropriate boundaries and good communication, which we discuss in the next chapters.

Our job is to do what Proverbs 4:23 says: "Above all else, guard your heart, for it is the wellspring of life." When we don't protect our hearts, they may close. Often guarding our hearts really means setting appropriate boundaries and allowing the space we need in a relationship to feel emotionally safe. If we want to "love one another deeply, from the heart" (1 Peter 1:22), we must discover why we close the door to our hearts and how to open it again (see 1 John 4:7-21).

This is extremely freeing. Instead of putting our efforts and energies into doing something we have zero ability to do (create love), we can focus on the state of our hearts: open or closed? We have control over our hearts. When we allow them to open to receive God's love, we can truly love our friends.

Ultimately, guarding our hearts means embracing them and accepting what they are experiencing in that moment. When I am hurt, I have learned to take a quiet step back to give myself some space, to become aware that my heart has closed. Sometimes I even tell myself, *Erin, your heart has closed and it is okay. It hurts when a friend speaks to you in that tone.* I then turn to the Lord and ask Him to work in my heart. I have found that when I do this rather than force myself back into the friendship immediately, my heart opens much sooner. Typically, this process lasts for less than twenty-four hours, and sometimes I can do it privately and carry on in the conversation or interaction.

The key to understanding why our hearts close in a relationship is to be clear about what is actually driving our hurts and pain, as well as the ways in which we haven't provided safety within our relationships. (See chapter 7 on communication skills that foster safety.) Often, we get stuck talking about an issue and not the core of what is going on deep under the surface. So what happens in our friendships that results in our hearts shutting down?

STOP PUSHING MY BUTTONS!

I vividly recall my heart closing toward a friend not long ago. I had been planning to go to the mall all by myself that morning. I finally had the day alone and was looking forward to it. I'd spent the week before "single parenting" while Greg had been out of town speaking. When he returned, he encouraged me to get out on my own. He knows what I need!

As I was heading out, I thought to myself, *Maybe Kathy would like to come with me.* Although I had been looking forward to going alone, at the last minute I decided I would enjoy some companionship.

So I dialed Kathy's number and she answered.

"Hi, Kathy, what are you up to? I'm running out to the mall and wanted to see if you'd like to come with me."

She paused for a minute. "Well, actually"—she hesitated— "I already have plans. I am going with Sally and Karen to the art festival."

I instantly felt "the feeling" deep within my chest. The phone call lasted a split second, and yet the ache was intense!

"All right," I answered disappointedly. "Have a good time, and I'll talk to you tomorrow."

I hung up the phone and stood there wondering, *What in the world is wrong with me?* I felt so left out and abandoned. You see, I was the one who had introduced these three women, and now they were doing things without me. The thought, *Is there something wrong with me that they don't want me with them?* was echoing throughout my head.

What made this so confusing was that on one level I was

perfectly fine with Kathy going to the art festival with our other friends. *I am an adult here,* I thought. *I'm not a jealous preteen!* However, this self-talk didn't do any good. It just made my feelings more intense. What was going on inside of me? I definitely wanted to understand this because I often felt this way—almost as if "buttons" inside of me had been pushed.

I am positive that most of us find ourselves in situations similar to this one. As women, we react strongly to pain within our friendships—even when someone isn't intending to hurt us.

What do you feel when your buttons are being pushed? What do you experience in your body when you feel left out, abandoned, rejected, or hurt by a friend? When you can identify what happens internally, you're on your way to recognizing what goes on deep in your heart.

When I'm hurt, I feel much like I've been punched in the stomach. I may or may not feel agitated; sometimes I just feel like shutting down and withdrawing from the person or situation. It might be different for you. Maybe you find it easiest to walk away from the relationship; at other times you may feel a whole lot better "letting the person have it." Sometimes you may give your friend the silent treatment or blame her for how you feel and your reaction to her. But regardless of how you respond when you've been hurt, your body's response is really a sign that your buttons are being pushed. Unfortunately, all these reactions can lead to the death of your friendship and create an unsafe environment for both parties involved.

You may be wondering—as I did the first time I heard about these "buttons"—what exactly we are talking about. We're not talking about belly buttons or buttons on your shirt but "fear buttons."

Learning about my buttons has changed my ability to know

and understand myself like few things have ever done. I now have more insight into my behaviors, such as why I withdraw, become agitated, and feel as if I've been punched.

There is another option to deal with this pain, one that is within our own personal control. This process begins with the decision to gain personal insight and understanding. And the critical part of this process comes when we gain insight into our hearts.

THE FEAR DANCE

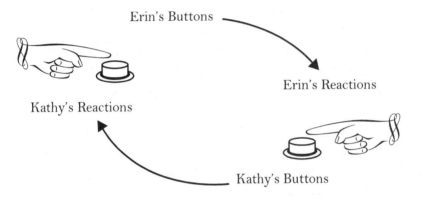

Every person has emotional fear buttons. Most people don't like to hear that. They may try to contradict this notion: "But I'm not afraid of anything. I feel perfectly safe in my home. I'm not afraid of my friends." That's good, but that isn't the kind of fear we're talking about. We mean things like the fear of being rejected, unloved, devalued, or alone. The concept of the Fear Dance was originally created at the Smalley Marriage Institute to describe the "dance" that often occurs between a husband and wife. Yet Gary Smalley's book *The DNA of Relationships* demonstrates that this dance occurs in all relationships—including those with coworkers, neighbors, and female friends.[4]

Identifying your fear buttons is important, because fear is the music that starts the dance—the Fear Dance. You would think that no one would purposely choose to participate in the Fear Dance. Surely most people would prefer to do a Love Dance or a Peace Dance, right? And yet it seems to be the default dance in most friendships. The only way to break the cycle is to recognize the Fear Dance and learn how to avoid it.

So how does the Fear Dance work? It begins when someone pushes your button, leading you to react with unhealthy words or actions calculated to motivate the other person to change and give you what you want. Often your reaction pushes the other person's button, who then reacts with unhealthy words or actions to try to get you to fulfill her wants. And suddenly the two of you end up in a full-blown Fear Dance.

To help you better understand the dance, let's take a closer look at the story I told in the beginning of this chapter.

Our buttons get pushed. At the very core of our conflicts are fear buttons. In other words, conflict is set in motion when our fear buttons get pushed. And we don't like it when this happens. You know what I'm talking about: When someone pushes your button, she has said or done something that makes you want to go after her or pull away from her.

The moment Kathy told me that she was going to the art festival with Sally and Karen, my buttons got pushed. In this case, the buttons that were pushed were my fears of being left out and rejected. I also felt that there must be something wrong with me that they didn't want me with them. Some other common fear buttons among women include anxieties about feeling alone, helpless, unworthy, disconnected, or unnecessary. What are some other emotional fear buttons, and what might they sound like in your friendship?

FEAR	WHAT THAT FEAR SOUNDS LIKE
Rejection	My friend doesn't want me; my friend doesn't need me; I'm not necessary in this relationship; I feel unwanted.
Abandonment	I will be alone; my friend will ultimately leave me; I will be left without any friends; my friend won't be committed to me for long; I will be deserted.
Disconnection	I will become emotionally detached or separated from my friend.
Helplessness/powerlessness . . .	I cannot do anything to change my friend or my situation; I do not possess the power, resources, capacity, or ability to get what I want; I will be controlled by my friend.
Defectiveness	Something is wrong with me; I'm the problem.
Inadequacy	I am not capable; I am incompetent.
Inferiority	Everyone else is better than I am; I am less valuable or important than others.
Invalidation	Who I am, what I think, what I do, or how I feel is not valued.
Being unloved	My friend doesn't like me anymore; my friendship lacks warm attachment, admiration, enthusiasm, or devotion.
Worthlessness/devaluation	I am useless; I have no value to my friend.
Not measuring up	I am never able to meet my friend's expectations; I am not good enough as a friend.
Not being accepted	My friend does not accept me; my friend is not pleased with me; my friend does not approve of me.
Judgment	I am always being unfairly judged or misjudged; my friend forms faulty or negative opinions about me; I am always being evaluated; my friend does not approve of me.
Being ignored	My friend will not pay attention to me; I will be unknown in my friendship; I feel neglected.
Unimportance	I am not important to my friend; I am irrelevant, insignificant, or of little priority to my friend.
Intimacy	I am afraid of opening up emotionally to my friend; I will be hurt emotionally if I allow my friend past my walls.

Being misunderstood .... My friend will fail to understand me correctly; she will get the wrong idea or impression about me; I will be misinterpreted or misread.

Misportrayal .... My friend has an inaccurate portrayal of me; I am misrepresented or represented in a false way; I am described in a negative or untrue manner; my friend paints a wrong picture of me; my friend has negative beliefs about me.

We react. Most people—consciously or unconsciously—fall into well-worn patterns of reacting when someone pushes their fear buttons. We'll do anything to soothe our hurt. We'll do anything to avoid the awful feeling. We'll do or say anything to calm our fears.

In fact, to deal with those fears, we have developed characteristic ways of reacting in order to protect ourselves. These "coping" reactions generally are an attempt to change the emotion and make the fear go away. The emotion becomes an enemy to conquer or avoid. Unfortunately, in that protected state, our hearts become closed behind our defense, which also tends to inadvertently close the door to intimacy. More often than not, such emotions and thinking result in behavior that damages relationships. When our fear buttons get pushed, we react.

Because I felt left out, rejected, and defective when talking with Kathy, I quickly withdrew from the conversation and disconnected by hanging up the phone. Of course, this pushed Kathy's buttons. She felt controlled and inadequate. Soon after our initial phone call, Kathy called back.

"Is everything okay?" she asked.

"I'm fine," I responded in a cold way. (Remember: *fine* means *f*eelings *i*nside *n*ot *e*xpressed!)

"Well"—Kathy hesitated—"it seems like you got awful quiet after I mentioned that I was going to the art festival with Sally and Karen. Did that bother you?"

"Not at all." (I wasn't being honest . . . if you couldn't tell!)

"Because we had planned this a long time ago," Kathy continued. "I actually thought you had something else going on or I would have invited you. So I didn't mean to hurt your feelings."

"Kathy," I stated, "I'm okay . . . really."

And that was the gist of our conversation.

Notice that once Kathy's buttons of feeling controlled and helpless had been pushed, she proceeded to defend and explain her actions to me. That's the dance! After our phone call, I felt more left out and rejected. Had we not hung up the phone, we probably would have cycled around a few times—our buttons would have been pushed and then we would have reacted again.

Did you notice that it's not so much the fears that disrupt and injure our relationships? It's how we choose to react when someone pushes our fear buttons. Most of us use unhealthy, faulty reactions to deal with our fear, and as a result we sabotage our friendships. Yet we can learn to respond appropriately rather than react emotionally.

If it's so destructive, why do we persist in doing the Fear Dance? While it may not be productive, sometimes it makes us feel better. Take what I did: withdrawal. Many women withdraw when their fear button gets pushed. They don't want to yell and scream, but they also don't want to allow their button to get pushed repeatedly. So what do they do? They make a quick exit and suddenly become unavailable. They may begin putting in more hours at work or become increasingly involved at their child's school.

However they do it, they take themselves out of the conflict by fleeing, either physically or emotionally. They're just trying to protect themselves—but they also harm the relationship and cause it to deteriorate. Rather than help a woman keep the peace and avoid conflict, withdrawal usually pushes our friend's buttons by tapping into her fear of disconnection.

Withdrawal, of course, is only one of the ways we react when our fear button gets pushed. The chart below shows some of the most common ways we react when we fear that our wants will not be met.[5]

REACTION	EXPLANATION
Withdrawal	I avoid others or alienate myself without resolution; I sulk or use the silent treatment.
Escalation	My emotions spiral out of control; I argue, raise my voice, or fly into a rage.
Belittling or sarcasm	I devalue or dishonor someone with words or actions; I call my friend names or take potshots at her.
Negative beliefs	I believe my friend is far worse than is really the case; I see my friend in a negative light or attribute negative motives to my friend.
Blaming	I place responsibility on others, not accepting fault; I'm convinced the problem is my friend's fault.
Exaggeration	I make overstatements or enlarge my words beyond bounds of the truth.
Tantrums	I have a fit of bad temper.
Denial	I refuse to admit the truth or reality.
Invalidation	I devalue my friend; I do not appreciate who my friend is or what she feels, thinks, or does.
Defensiveness	Instead of listening, I defend myself by providing an explanation.
Clingyness	I develop a strong emotional attachment or dependence on my friend.
Passive-aggressive behavior	I display negative emotions, resentment, and aggression in passive ways, such as procrastination and stubbornness.
Caretaking	I become responsible for others by giving physical or emotional care and support to the point that I am doing too much for my friend.

Acting out.	I engage in negative behaviors such as drug or alcohol abuse, excessive shopping, or overeating.
Overfunctioning	I do what others should be doing and take responsibility for my friend.
Going into fix-it mode	I focus almost exclusively on what is needed to solve the problem.
Complaining	I express unhappiness or make accusations.
Aggression or abuse.	I become verbally or physically aggressive, possibly abusive.
Manipulation.	I control my friend for my own advantage.
Anger and rage	I display strong feelings of displeasure or violent, uncontrolled emotions.
Catastrophizing.	I use dramatic, exaggerated expressions to depict that the friendship is in danger or that it has failed.
Numbing out.	I become devoid of emotion, or I have no regard for my friend's needs or troubles.

The Fear Dance works with guaranteed "success" every time it goes into motion. It doesn't matter what starts it; it works perfectly to get us right where we don't want to be. And it does so every single time. Interestingly, we engage in the Fear Dance with a worthy goal: At some level we want to keep the relationship going. In that way, such a system could be called "functionally dysfunctional."

So the Fear Dance is functional in that it keeps two people interacting, even though that interaction consistently hurts. It functions in a painful, crazy kind of way. Yet it's deeply dysfunctional and will never lead to the kind of friendship we really want.

The worst thing about the Fear Dance is that it sets up two friends as adversaries and makes their friendship feel very unsafe. Any time we feel unsafe in a relationship, our hearts will close and we will disconnect. Other problems with the Fear Dance are these:

1. It can last a lifetime. People can argue about the same thing for more than twenty years.
2. In the dance, we deal with surface issues rather than with the core issues.
3. Actually, the issues don't even matter. People will dance the same no matter what causes the conflict.
4. Our natural first instinct is to react when our buttons are pushed rather than to respond. Remember Adam in the Garden? After God confronted him, Genesis 3:10 reports: Adam said, "I heard you in the garden, and I was afraid because I was naked; so I hid."
5. The Fear Dance creates codependency. Our focus is on what our friend should do, making us feel powerless. We fall into a trap that leads us to think, My friend's job is to make me feel . . . So we attempt to manipulate our friend to get her to attend to our wants and desires. We believe that we will feel better if she does what we want. Ultimately, we see our friend as both the problem and solution. This is what creates the codependency. God didn't create us to be self-reliant, and as human beings we naturally gravitate toward being dependent. But there's a problem: God created us so that our deepest needs can be met by Him alone, not by our friends, our bosses, or even our spouses. So although the Fear Dance "works" in a way, it cannot bring us to where we want to be.
6. The dance leads us to talk or argue about things that are a total waste of time (e.g., who's right and wrong, who's to blame, who should solve it).

As the primary motivator for behavior, fear frequently colors the way we live and react to life. Our fears can take many forms, including anxiety, stress, dread, defensiveness, and avoidance. Our fears are often irrational, and our fear-based behaviors often lead us to develop life strategies and reactions that carry numerous unfortunate consequences. Many times we let fear stop us from doing what we want and need to do.

So is there anything about our fear buttons that can contribute to deep, grown-up relationships? Surprisingly, the answer is yes. As an emotion, fear can be a useful source of information, and acknowledging and discussing our fears can open the door to intimate moments with our friends. When Kathy called back, I could have been honest with her about my heart, without making her feel responsible for the way I was feeling. I might have said, "After giving it some thought, I realized I was feeling left out and rejected when I heard that the three of you were going to the art show without me. I felt as if maybe something was wrong with me and that's why I hadn't been included. I want you to know, though, that these are issues I'm trying to work through with God's help. You're not responsible for how I feel."

Kathy then would have had the opportunity to express her concern about my perceptions by asking questions and seeking more information. Being vulnerable enough to share our fears with a female friend opens the door to sharing, compassion, understanding, and love—in other words, emotional intimacy. Ultimately, this is what we want as women. Nothing will connect us to another person more than taking time to care and offer compassion as she works through painful emotions. Remember, though, we need to be careful not to assume responsibility for another's feelings.

On a personal level, learning to acknowledge and understand what the fear reveals about our needs and beliefs provides an opportunity to care for ourselves emotionally, physically, spiritually, and mentally. Knowing ourselves—and letting others know us—is critical to maintaining an open heart, one that is capable of receiving and giving love. And that is another mark of a grown-up friendship.

The grown-up girlfriend...

... allows her heart to open to receive God's love so she can truly love her friends as He intended.

. . . .

REFLECTION QUESTIONS

1. What is one thing you learned from this chapter about the importance of your heart? Some Scriptures that point to the importance of our hearts are listed on page 56–57. Search God's Word for other verses that describe the importance of the heart.

2. What has been your theory on giving and receiving love? Do you agree that the capacity to love others comes from the Lord and that we don't create it ourselves? Why or why not?

3. Can you identify your primary fear button? Can you identify your most common reactions to fear?

4. Describe a recent scenario in which you felt the Fear Dance take over. Can you attempt to identify what buttons were pushed in you? Could you talk to your friend about what buttons might have been pushed in her?

5

$\mathscr{T}$HE GROWN-UP FRIEND SETS AND RESPECTS BOUNDARIES

[Carrie]

A true friend sympathizes freely, advises justly,
assists readily, adventures boldly, takes all
patiently, defends courageously and
continues a friend unchangeably.
WILLIAM PENN

Sonia and her friend Emily have been friends since college. They have married, had children, walked through some trials, and shared fun and laughter and Jesus. Sonia describes this relationship as one in which she is "known" and can share her heart and feel needed. Though she describes it as safe, she wonders at times if that is really true.

You see, she feels a bit uneasy when Emily questions her or asks her for information that she doesn't feel comfortable sharing, such as intimate details about her husband. Also, Emily is very open with her opinion on most things—sometimes even when Sonia hasn't asked for it. Sonia has also noticed that Emily isn't always as receptive to hearing her opinions. Emily isn't completely satisfied with their relationship either. At times she feels that Sonia is uptight and puts a wall up, keeping Emily out or keeping their hearts from totally connecting.

This friendship continues because at the core these two really do love each other and appreciate their basket one friendship, but they have never really navigated the issue of healthy, godly boundaries. They have not learned how to talk about them, how to identify what is comfortable for each of them, and how to keep boundaries in place. They have not always taken care of their hearts well.

Proverbs 4:23 tells us to guard our hearts because they are the wellspring of life—everything flows out of them, including our friendships, no matter what basket they fall into or what purpose they have. In the last chapter, Erin talked about one way we guard our hearts—by being aware of our "fear buttons" and preventing our hearts from closing when they've been hurt. In this chapter, I want to explore another way to guard our hearts: by setting boundaries.

Boundaries. That's not a new word or concept for many. Most of us think of boundaries as imaginary lines that define where each of us begins as a unique human being, including the totality of our emotions, intellect, spirituality, and physical bodies. We develop boundaries over the course of our lifetimes as we develop our identities and understand more thoroughly who God has created us to be.

Boundaries were definitely God's idea. In Mark 12:30-31 we are commanded to love the Lord our God with all our hearts, souls, minds, and strength and to love our neighbors as ourselves. If we are to love with open hearts, then this healthy, authentic love must emanate from a heart that is well protected with godly boundaries. "The good man brings good things out of the good stored up in his heart, and the evil man brings evil things out of the evil stored up in his heart. For out of the overflow of his heart his mouth speaks" (Luke 6:45).

A woman with good boundaries honors both her own heart

and her friend's heart. When good boundaries are in place, two people are drawn to each other and feel a sense of safety. In his book *The Inner Voice of Love*, Henri Nouwen puts it this way: "When you claim for yourself the power over your drawbridge [the boundary of your heart], you will discover new joy and peace in your heart and find yourself able to share that joy and peace with others."[1]

A WOMAN'S DILEMMA

We know that women desire to need and be needed. When we try to set limits or protect our hearts, we often get fearful or anxious. For instance, I like to share my opinion openly and have had to learn to keep quiet and listen more often so that I do not invade others' hearts. I also do not like conflict, so it is difficult to set boundaries with those who step on my heart. These struggles are probably pretty typical for you too.

Because we are wired to bond and connect, we females can really stink at boundaries! We need to understand how boundaries protect our hearts and then take action to begin to change in this area. Perhaps you grew up in difficult circumstances that discouraged you from setting boundaries. If you haven't already done so, I encourage you to pursue healing from any wounds from the past that affect your present relationships, including the ability to set healthy boundaries. See a counselor, talk to a mentor, study grief and loss, and allow the loving Father to enter your wounded heart and heal it. Begin by believing that the Lord can provide healing and show you how to protect your delicate and precious heart. Remember, relationships are God's idea, and He has a purpose for your friendships. For that reason, He wants to help us learn to set good boundaries.

Emotional Boundaries

Healthy boundaries help us with several heart issues. First, they help us with our emotions. Most of us fall into one of two categories: Either we are emotionally stuck or we allow our emotions to overwhelm us and those around us. When we guard our hearts with appropriate boundaries, we begin to be aware of our hearts in much more discerning ways. We notice our sadness, our anger, our fear, our disappointment, our disillusionment, and so on. As we become familiar and comfortable with our hearts, the core of who we are, we can better discern how to name and share our emotions with others.

I have a wonderful husband and three very cool sons. Each one of us came into this world with a unique and individual personality; therefore, we do not experience our emotions alike. A few of us (myself included) have a tendency to get worked up when we are feeling emotional, and those around us get the fallout. We call it "having a moment of hysteria." In developing healthy boundaries, we must get better at understanding our emotions and expressing them at times and in ways most helpful to us and our friend. Often that means processing emotions before sharing them. For example, when we get angry, we need to figure out where our anger is coming from before we express it. We cannot expect someone else to understand our emotions when we don't really understand them well ourselves.

Once we understand our emotions, we can express them appropriately. One way to do this is to say, "I am feeling angry [lonely/sad], and I just wanted you to know this and pray for me." We are less likely to cross someone's emotional boundary if we take the time to do this.

Establishing healthy boundaries also protects us from overreacting when our friend's emotions are out of control. It prevents us from being manipulated by friends who dump their emotions on us, expecting us to fix them.

Not everyone in my family gets overly emotional. Others have a difficult time naming their emotion, let alone allowing it to come out. Their job is to begin figuring out the emotions they're feeling and some godly, safe ways of expressing them. When responding to others, they don't need to shrink back out of fear that they will be expected to "fix" everything; instead, they can simply say, "I'm sorry and wish it could be better." They can then ask if there is anything they can do and pray for the discernment to know whether that person's request is something Jesus wants them to do.

One way to grow in this area is to ask your friends for feedback on how you deal with or process your emotions. Only do this with those you trust to be tender and honest. Handling, expressing, understanding, and processing emotions with good boundaries around the heart increases the health of a relationship.

Developing healthy boundaries around emotions can help us with our expectations as well. Only one person can fully hold our emotions, and that is Jesus. I cannot expect all my loved ones to know and understand every emotion I feel, though I can hope they will desire to hold my emotions safely. Walking through this cancer has taught me much about expressing emotions in godly and helpful ways. When I am disappointed or feel my friend or my husband does not understand, I've come to realize and accept that they probably don't! Be patient and be committed to this process of discovering your emotional heart and setting good boundaries.

Physical Boundaries

Second, boundaries of the heart protect us physically. We could not write this book without addressing the physical aspect of a relationship between two women. As women, we often have the desire to be affectionate, and this desire is something precious built into our DNA. I love the scene from the movie *Someone Like You* in which Jane, played by Ashley Judd, gets the call from her brother-in-law that her sister, Alice, has had a miscarriage and is at the hospital. Jane goes to the hospital and crawls directly into the little twin bed with her sister. She wraps her in her arms and holds her. Alice cries and shares her pain of not getting to see the baby or having the chance to watch her husband play ball with him someday. Jane just continues to hold her, listening, crying a few tears, and brushing her hair from her face.

Here is the best part! Alice's husband, Stephen, comes into the room after getting ice and water for his wife. He wants to do whatever he can for her. Alice just looks at him and says, "Isn't he the best? I love him so much." The affection is tender. Yet Jane is the one who knows just what her sister needs and how to support her. Neither sister expects the husband to function as they do, and they appreciate his efforts to meet Alice's needs the best way he knows how. However, sometimes another woman, through her touch and silent presence, offers just what we need.

I know this from my own experience. Almost a year after my cancer diagnosis, I received an unsettling call. I was on my way to a shopping trip with my mom while we were in Phoenix together. The nurse on the other end of the line told me that an MRI showed a small lesion on my spine and said I would need to go to MD Anderson Cancer Center in Houston, where I was receiving my care, for ten days of radiation therapy. I got off the phone and cried. My mother, who typically is not overly affectionate, took my hand and held it. She cried with me until I was done. She said that she was sorry and knew that this hurt but that she would be there to help me through it in any way she could. I was tired and weary from the process of this cancer journey with its twists and turns. I did not really know what I was feeling, so just having my hand held quietly by my mom was so right. It is now a treasured memory.

On another occasion my friend Cheryl, during the year she watched her brother walk through and eventually die of lung cancer, just put her head on my shoulder during a church service. I took her hand. We sat and listened to worship and held each other emotionally in her weariness. These are all precious examples of appropriate affection and boundaries around the heart.

As women, we often go looking for other women to fill our emotional tanks. If we're not careful, however, we can also look to them to fill our needs for affection in ways that are inappropriate. We live in a day and age in which sex is the primary way our culture portrays connection with others. I have counseled numerous women who started out in friendships that felt safe but who did not have the emotional awareness or the ability to express their affection in healthy ways. Often they ended up having sexual contact with their friends. This led to tremendous shame and guilt, as well as a distancing from their loving heavenly Father.

Here are some questions that might raise red flags and let you know that you need to establish better physical boundaries to guard the way you give and receive affection.

1. If you are married, are you unhappy with the affection level in your marriage? Do you look to your friends to fill that for you?
2. Whether you are married or not, do your friends often tell you that they're unhappy about the lack of affection in their lives?

3. Have either you or your friend been sexually abused in the past?
4. Do some of your friends express uneasiness about the way you show affection? Do they tell you that you engulf and overwhelm them with your physical advances?

I would encourage you to talk with someone if you feel you or your friend is in danger of crossing a physical boundary. When counseling, I have often found that poor physical boundaries result from a wounded heart or a person's attempt to get her deepest needs met from another person rather than God, who is really the only one who ultimately can satisfy those needs.

The ability to be appropriately affectionate is priceless. I have had to learn to be more affectionate because the boundaries I built around my heart growing up were too tight. Women who do this may believe that nobody really wants to touch us because we grew up in homes where affection wasn't expressed often. I thank God for my tender husband and the friends who have taken the first step to hug me or reach out to me. They have enabled me to be more affectionate. I have learned even more in my broken state of walking through cancer. I treasure every loving hand and hug and tear that says, "I love you and will walk this journey with you the best I can."

What about you? Do you isolate your heart, or do you cling too tightly to your friends and then walk away disappointed when they don't meet your needs? Are you in a relationship that doesn't honor God through your physical expressions of affection? Oh, this is important, dear women. Affection is too great a gift not to experience it in the way God intended. Pray about it, look for ways to touch if you tend to hold back, and consider how to receive touch appropriately.

BOUNDARIES THAT PROTECT
OUR IDENTITIES

Last, boundaries help us to recognize that we are different from our friends and enable us to define who we are. As women, we so long to connect that we must guard against sacrificing our identities to do so. When we have good boundaries, we are able to be the women God created us to be, unique and different from our friends.

What does this mean? If we're not careful, we end up either isolating ourselves from other people or engulfing them in an attempt to become that other person. Neither approach leads to a healthy friendship, and our hearts get lost in the process. As we grow more comfortable with our own identities in Christ, we no longer need to either hide our opinions or force them on others; instead, we learn proper ways to communicate our thoughts and ideas. Two friends who can trust each other to share their thoughts and opinions without forcing them on the other have developed healthy intimacy.

How do we know if we have an inappropriate boundary in this area? We may struggle to get our own way and not be open to hearing another's thoughts or opinions. Conversely, if we are absolutely unaware of our own identity, we may agree with another person frequently, avoid conflict, follow her lead, and repress our own opinions. Undifferentiated people over-agree or overargue; they react emotionally with defiance or submissiveness. They are easily moved to emotionality. This undifferentiated experience can set us up for the destructive relationships talked about in chapter 9.

On the other hand, differentiation is the ability to think and reflect, not respond automatically. When I understand that I am different from my friend, I communicate in wiser ways. I also set the boundaries I need and can appreciate my personality as being different from hers. I can separate my thoughts and feelings from hers, which means, for instance, that if she gets angry I do not have to take that on by getting angry in response.

The key to accepting our own identity is remembering that Christ created each one of us uniquely, with a specific purpose for our lives in mind (see Psalm 139). This is where we must begin, because if we don't know who we are created to be in Christ, how can we reflect that to another person? As we come to understand that Christ dwells in our hearts, we take on His personality and character. Our friends then see an authentic, humble, honest human being who is comfortable with herself. Only when we understand how we are different from others can we really identify the purpose of our friendships.

In addition, we are better equipped to respond when our friends behave in hurtful ways. We learn that others' anxiety does not need to raise our own. For example, we don't need to personalize what someone says and assume it is intended to hurt us. When we think first rather than have an immediate emotional reaction, we can ask questions to clarify what our friend is communicating. Rather than accusing her with a "you" statement, such as, "You seem upset with me," we can diffuse tension with "I" statements, such as, "I want to understand you and need clarification on what you're saying." That lets your friend know you are trying to understand her rather than personalizing her words.

Sometimes when we're communicating, we make another's issue our problem or make a problem where one didn't even exist. This can be prevented by keeping our emotions under control and seeking more information in nonthreatening ways. When we seek to understand our friend, we are less likely to get anxious and defensive. Henri Nouwen says it so beautifully in *The Inner Voice of Love*:

> *The great task is to claim yourself for yourself, so that you can contain your needs within the boundaries of your self and hold them in the presence of those you love. True mutuality in love requires people who possess themselves and who can give to each other while holding on to their own identities. So, in order both to give more effectively and to be more self-contained with your needs, you must learn to set boundaries to your love.*[2]

A BOUNDARY OF LOVE

The Lord loves the heart. He created our hearts with such compassionate, discerning care. He protects the heart when we allow Him to, and He guides and directs our hearts. His heart longs to connect to ours, and in that connection we will discover and live the most healthy boundaries we can possibly experience on this earth.

I saw this illustrated in an interesting way when Gary and I were staying at a hotel in Scottsdale, Arizona, while in town to speak at a conference. Did you know that certain plants close up during the times when they will not be protected? One such plant grows in Arizona. At night when we opened our patio, we smelled an incredible fragrance. We could never smell it during the day, however. Finally we began watching the bush outside our door and noticed that the flowers opened only at night so as not to be damaged by the hot sun. Our hearts are a bit like those flowers. Boundaries around our hearts help them to flourish in the most healthy ways, giving life to our souls and intimacy to our relationships. May you be full of life as you develop boundaries of the heart!

The grown-up girlfriend...

... sets healthy boundaries that enable her to better understand and appropriately express her emotions and needs.

. . . .

REFLECTION QUESTIONS

1. What are some areas of your heart that you either protect or expose too much?

2. If you were to allow God a little further into your heart, what would that look like? How would your life be different?

3. How would you describe yourself in the differentiation process? If you are not very well differentiated, what do you think needs to change?

4. What is one way you could change in the next month so that you would have more healthy, godly boundaries of the heart?

6

*T*HE GROWN-UP FRIEND
EMBRACES DIFFERENCES

[Carrie]

*Your best friend is the person who brings
out the best that is within you.*
HENRY FORD

Disagreements are one of the best ways we grow.
WILLIAM AND PATRICIA COLEMAN[1]

*I am glad for who you are, not what
I want you to become.*
WILLIAM AND PATRICIA COLEMAN[2]

*A successful relationship is built when
two people are striving to become the
best-version-of-themselves, challenging and
encouraging each other to become the
best-version-of-themselves, and inspiring others
to pursue their essential purpose by the
example of their lives and their love.*
MATTHEW KELLY

I have had a sense of being "different" since I was a small
child. My family are dear people. I love my dad, my mom, and
my two sisters, but I always felt like the "different" one, truly
the odd one out! I wanted more social activity and would have

enjoyed more sleepovers and parties. I wondered why nobody ever stayed with us. I also liked talking *a lot*. I could tell this particularly annoyed my dad at times. I heard him say over and over again, "Carrie, do you always have to have the last word?" I remember thinking, *Well, somebody has to say something around here!*

I look back and see I was the one who cried more openly and desired more affection. I always had many friendships going, and now I have friends across the country since I've moved a number of times. I became a counselor. That is very different from who the rest of my family is.

You also may have felt different growing up and wondered if you were normal. What I did not understand as a child is that we are created uniquely and bring these differences to our world of relationships. Sometimes this is positive, but sometimes our differences, when not understood and embraced, can produce negative results, such as frustration and unresolved, unhealthy conflict.

WHEN THINGS GET CONFUSING!

Marcia and Kathy enjoy their friendship but at times feel some lingering tension. Marcia enjoys alone time with Kathy, but Kathy frequently brings along at least a couple of other friends when she and Marcia meet for lunch or coffee. In addition to this annoyance, Kathy rarely tells Marcia she has invited other people. Kathy walks away energized by all the activity, but Marcia usually feels drained by the group and disrespected by Kathy. Kathy gets frustrated when she asks Marcia what she is thinking and Marcia answers, "I don't know." Kathy likes to verbally process her life with Marcia but notices that Marcia rarely does that with her. This gives Kathy a sense that she does not know Marcia as well as she would like to.

Pam and Deb are different as well. Pam loves to dream about the future. She never runs out of ideas and loves to talk about what she and Deb could do down the road, whether traveling, starting a ministry, or writing a book. Deb prefers to concentrate on the present day. She loves the details of the moment. Pam sometimes gets bored with her day and goes into dreaming mode. Deb has a hard time getting Pam to nail down the details and often responds very literally to Pam's dreaming mode. If Pam says they should plan a trip to the beach for a weekend, Deb thinks that Pam means "Let's plan it," so she begins the planning process. Two days later Pam may have forgotten she even mentioned the beach! Deb feels misunderstood.

Karen is never on time and runs life by the moment. She loves the adrenaline of the "last-minute rush." In college she would write her twenty-page paper the night before it was due and still get an A on it. She is spontaneous and loves to have fun, so fun takes precedence over work! She keeps a calendar by her desk only because she likes the pictures. Her friend Joyce is very structured. In college the twenty-page paper was done two weeks in advance of the due date. Joyce completes her work before she plays, and for her "on time" means arriving ten minutes before the appointment. Despite their differences, these two ladies love each other! Joyce was drawn to Karen's spontaneity, and she marvels that Karen manages to remember and actually make it to her appointments. However, Joyce does get frustrated when she has to wait and wait for Karen or when Karen drops their plans because something "more fun" comes up.

These are just a few examples showing how differences in our personalities and approaches to life can really put the heat on our friendships. The key, as we will talk about, is to accept that we are different from each other and that we were probably drawn together because of our differences. To bring out the best in each other, we have to be willing to let go of our need to change our friend and instead acknowledge and address unmet expectations and frustrations as they occur. Embracing differences means we accept how God has created us. This is so exciting when we truly get it! It is at this point that we are less bothered by our dissimilarities and realize we don't have to change, though we might choose to make allowances for one another or modify our behavior in order to be more lovable to our friend.

YOU'VE GOT PERSONALITY

There are several different ways to look at personality types and preferences.[3] For our purposes, we will talk generally about some of the major differences between people and how to mesh these differences in friendships. When we talk about aspects of personality, we are not trying to put people into boxes but rather are talking about some common ways humans look at the world and then organize and structure their lives. We'll also be looking at how we take in information and make decisions.

One difference between people in my family showed up when my son Nathan was about two or three. Gary and I began to notice that big groups of people would overwhelm him, and birthday parties were sometimes a disaster. He would get frustrated when we asked him to verbalize things. Both Gary and I are extroverts, and Nathan is an introvert. Extroverted personalities tend to get their energy from being with people and from their surroundings. Extroverts enjoy using words to figure out what they are thinking, so they like to bounce ideas off their friends verbally. Too much alone time may suck energy from the extrovert.

Introverts think privately and usually come to a decision

before saying much. They enjoy a few friends and get energy from alone time. In the example of Marcia and Kathy, Marcia is the introvert and Kathy is the extrovert. Kathy loves a party and having several people together at once, while Marcia enjoys the alone time with Kathy. Kathy gets frustrated with Marcia because she feels she does not know what Marcia is thinking, while Kathy tells Marcia about her feelings and thoughts freely and frequently.

I prefer extroversion just as I prefer to use my right hand, but my extroversion will look just a little bit different from yours if you are an extrovert. Another way to look at this is that I do not prefer introversion like I do not prefer to use my left hand. I can use my left hand and I can experience introversion, but I truly prefer extroversion. Knowing this about myself is helpful as I relate to the introverted people in my life.

Dreamers and detailers also differ in significant ways. This is the source of much of the tension in Pam and Deb's friendship. I am a detailed person and like living in the present. I don't mind planning, but I have to work at brainstorming. Those who are big-picture people, like my husband, Gary, live for dreaming about the future, whether their ideas come true or not. They are not very present and sometimes might seem distracted. To the detail person, this may feel disrespectful. In my relationship with Gary, I see him as the kite and myself as the string that keeps him from flying off to the galaxies beyond! Usually the detail person excels at raining on the parade of the big-picture person, so I have had to learn much about letting loose and taking time to dream a little. I love to think and contemplate, but dreaming is a whole other experience that God designed for us. Conversely, enjoying the present is such a wonderful gift, and the dreamer could do well to notice what is happening right now in the present moment so she doesn't miss God's current blessing.

Another major difference in personality shows up in the way we structure our world—or don't structure it! Some people just want to have fun, and their lists, daily planners, and calendars are toys rather than something to structure their lives. They just like to wait to see how the week unfolds. Other people make lists and plan their days in advance.

People who are late will probably always be late, and those of us who like to be on time (which really means early) will continue to be frustrated by the late people. The nonstructured person is usually easy to be around but can bring a feeling of chaos to the structured person. We structured people are always trying to get those nonstructured people organized, so we may come across as controlling to them. In my family we have three structured people and a couple of spontaneous sons. It makes for an interesting life.

I have a dear friend who organizes her life very differently from mine. When I visit her, we bounce from one thing to the next, which isn't my preferred way to structure my days. However, the joy that she finds in life, along with her smile and excitement about the next exciting thing we might encounter, has come to bring me joy. Unlike her, even if I don't have a big agenda for the day, I have a sense of what needs to be done and will follow that map pretty well—though I've learned to be open to change. That has happened with age! Walking through cancer has caused me to give up some of my need for a lot of lists and agendas as well. I've discovered that crisis truly will make a person flexible.

Finally, people differ in how they make decisions. Some base their decisions on rational thought. Others make decisions based on their emotions and how they think the decision will affect their relationships. Statistically, a higher percentage of women are feelers, but every now and then a woman may be a thinker when it comes to making decisions. This difference can cause conflict in a friendship. We feelers get our feelings hurt, often by thinkers, who can be blunt and think in terms of the bottom line. On the other hand, thinkers get frustrated with us feelers and think we take things too personally. I have learned a great deal by being married to my thinker husband. I do like rational thought but have a tendency to personalize things he says that are not intended to hurt me. Melanie sometimes feels as if her friend Dana misses her heart, while Dana thinks Melanie often fails to look at the facts. Dana is slowly learning to ask Melanie how she is feeling when they have a conflict or even when Melanie has to make a big decision that has nothing to do with their relationship. Only then will Dana ask if Melanie wants her input. Melanie is coming to appreciate Dana's ability to make difficult decisions, even at the risk of compromising harmony.

IDENTIFY PURPOSE IN THE MIDST OF DIFFERENCES

No doubt about it—the different ways our friends approach life can be irritating to us. Yet this is another occasion when understanding that God has a purpose for our friendships can be so liberating. By taking the time to understand our personality differences and embracing the uniqueness of our friends, we can see more clearly why God has brought us together. When we come to understand each other and work through our frustrations, we create an incredible reflection of Christ and His love.

In the year before Amy married our son Nathan, she worked with Gary and me at the Center for Relationship Enrichment at John Brown University. She was actually offered the job before we even knew these two had a "thing" going! Amy and I worked to create and establish the center's University Relationships Initiative, a program designed to prepare students to build healthy relationships during college and beyond. Once Nathan and Amy became engaged, she and I felt the purpose of our relationship was twofold: to successfully establish the initiative and to deepen our relationship as soon-to-be-family members. It was a dear and precious year of my life. I will never forget it.

After the wedding Nathan and Amy moved to Denver, where he attended Denver Seminary. For the first several weeks after they moved, I would walk into the center and see Amy's empty office next to mine. I cried almost every day for a while. God had done such a work in our relationship that we were grounded for life as second mother (she calls me Mom) and daughter. She also had become a good and trusted friend.

While Amy and I have fairly similar personalities, we still had to navigate some conflict and frustrations while working together. She is a little more structured than I am, and I am actually more of a big-picture person than she is (thanks to what I have learned from the big-picture people in my life). When we worked together, Amy assumed that once we had met on an issue, our decisions were final and she could proceed with an unchanging plan from then on. However, at times I would continue processing after our meetings and come up with another approach to achieving our goals.

That could be frustrating to Amy, especially when she had begun working on the details of our plan. I learned to let her know when I was still considering the big picture. We then brainstormed ideas, and when we finished that process, she zeroed in on the details and did so far better than I ever could. Eventually we learned to laugh at our differences, and today we have a close relationship.

Can you think of a friend who sometimes annoys you just because of how she does things? Maybe she always arrives at your lunch dates late. Maybe she turns glassy-eyed when you start talking about your dream to write the great American novel. Perhaps she talks so much you take a few aspirin before getting together to stave off the inevitable headache. What about that friend who seems to have one emotional crisis after another? If you have a friend who can drive you up the wall, ask yourself, *What might the Lord be trying to accomplish by pulling together two women with such different personalities?* No doubt God is growing you individually through your friendship, but there is probably a bigger purpose that will benefit His Kingdom as well. In Scripture, the Lord commands us to be gentle, kindhearted, and understanding—to learn how to love well. The fact that we are different from one another gives us the perfect opportunity to develop those virtues. Loving well means learning to embrace differences.

If you and a friend experience frequent conflict, consider meeting to discuss your differences and ways those differences could draw you together instead of driving you apart. I find it helpful to praise my friends in the areas that they are different from me and to see their personalities as gifts rather than annoyances. So often we become angry or hurt just because our friend approaches the world differently than we do. Imagine the alternative: a world full of little clones. Not very appealing, is it?

THE VALUE OF DIFFERENCES

Ever notice how often we associate the word *wrong* with the word *different*? Think about it. Rarely does *different* have a positive meaning! It usually means weird, out of the norm, or just plain wrong. I challenge you, though, to look at differences as being *valuable*! When we see how we are different and understand our personalities and those of our friends, we can begin to modify our expectations of them. When they frustrate us, we so often want to jump in and change them. However, when we don't expect our friend to approach the world as we do, we can begin to appreciate her uniqueness. I remember telling my friend Karen, the spontaneous, creative, last-minute-rush friend, just how much fun she is. She adds sparkle to life. See? A more structured person like me can choose to look at the "sparkle" of a spontaneous personality type instead of calling it "chaotic"! On the other hand, Karen and others like her can look at structured people and appreciate the order and structure we provide rather than labeling us "uptight." Reframing personality differences in this way really helps us get perspective and keeps us focused on the purpose of our friendship.

In the big picture of life, who really cares if we are late! While going through cancer treatment at MD Anderson in Houston, I have learned that an appointment time really means appointment day. Patients are assigned a time just to make sure they show up on the right day. Waiting has become something I can now do well. I wait on appointments, I wait in airports, and right now as I am away from home for three weeks of radiation treatments, I am waiting to go home. I do not have control over my schedule, and rarely can I make up an agenda and really follow it. I so appreciate what God has taught me through this. Giving up control can be the structured person's nightmare come true, or she can choose to appreciate the freedom it brings when circumstances are beyond her control.

That's not to say that being different from one another is always easy or an obvious blessing! The key to dealing with differences is the willingness to take time to understand our friend and to affirm her in who she is. We must also let go of our need to change her into someone she is not. If we are constantly in the "I want to understand you" mode rather than in the "You are wrong and need to change" mode, something radical happens to the relationship. Instead of telling Gary that he is way out there with some of his dreams, I have, on occasion, said, "I hope for you that your dream will come true." This appreciation for his differences forces me to stop focusing on what I want and to appreciate the strengths he brings to my life.

Though I've mentioned that I'm an extrovert, as I have grown older I have felt a need for more introvert time. I even will take time to think before the words come out! I have learned this from my introverted friends, and it has been good for me. I have also learned to be spontaneous and do some brainstorming when I need to think about what the big picture might be concerning a project or a conflict. All these styles are the opposite of my natural preferences. I believe that navigating, understanding, and embracing differences rather than fighting them makes us better people, better friends, and in the end, more Christlike. Don't misunderstand: The goal is not to acquire every possible facet of personality but rather to be able to use some facets that are uncomfortable.

BELIEVING IN THE POWER OF DIFFERENCES GROWS US UP

*Just as each of us has one body with many members,
and these members do not all have the same
function, so in Christ we who are many form one
body, and each member belongs to all the others.*

ROMANS 12:4-5

Do we really believe this? If we did, we would interact with others in a radically different way. Truly, we would be much less annoyed and frustrated each day. Keep track of how many times today someone irritates you. I can be annoyed many, many times in one day, beginning with my husband and sons! Yet when I accept that God has formed us as a body and we all have unique roles to fill, I understand that we need each other to function properly. If our first thoughts toward someone are negative or critical, guess what? They will almost surely annoy us! We have power over our thoughts! We can choose perspective. It's true.

I once had to ask a friend her forgiveness for not accepting her introversion in the past. Now when my friend, who is more introverted than I am, is not ready to share her emotions because she is still thinking or processing them, my first thought or reaction isn't automatically, *Oh, she is just keeping things inside* or *She doesn't trust me with her emotions.* Instead, I've come to understand her need for space. I need to honor her and respect the way she relates to the world. She now knows I accept her for who she is. That has drawn us closer together—even more so than if we told each other all our emotions. Acceptance is a powerful bonding agent.

Acceptance communicates love, support, encouragement, understanding, and trust. When I communicate disapproval and suggest that a friend needs to change, I am actually questioning who she is at her core. Be careful. Even when we make fun of or tease each other about differences, we are communicating nonacceptance, thus undermining trust and intimacy.

Acceptance is a great place to start in the grown-up friendship. It does not mean that you and your friends should never talk about your differences. What is important is that when you do talk, be sure you are encouraging of each other's personality. Use the "I" statement approach and give each other freedom. An example would look like this: "Friend, I'm an extrovert, so I would love to hear more from your heart—what you feel and what you want and like and desire. Sometimes I feel like I miss out on that aspect of our relationship. It's important, though, that this is something you want and are comfortable with and have freedom in. If you are not comfortable with it, then that is okay. I also want to know if I overwhelm you at times with my words. If I do, I want to do that differently."

Be careful to avoid using your personality preferences as excuses for behavior that is not godly or helpful. If I am an extrovert, I could blurt out angry- or accusing-sounding statements and then say something like, "That's just the way I am." This is not acceptable. We are never to use our personalities to manipulate or control another person. Likewise, a friend who is unwilling to appreciate who we are or who expects us to function just like her may not be open to growing. While difficult, we must acknowledge this conflict and seek resolution. If that is impossible, we may decide to let the friendship go. (See chapter 10 for more on this difficult topic.)

Psychologist and author Michael P. Nichols sums up what I mean about accepting differences in ourselves and our friends:

> *If we are to have the courage to be ourselves, to stand squarely on our own two feet, then we must accept and acknowledge that other people are themselves and entitled to their own unique points of view. The idea is not to distance ourselves from others but to let them be themselves while we continue to be ourselves. . . . Trying harder to understand the other person's perspective takes effort, but it isn't just a skill to be studied and practiced. Hearing someone is an expression of caring enough to listen.*[4]

The grown-up girlfriend . . .

. . . doesn't expect her friend to approach the world as she does but appreciates her uniqueness.

. . . .

REFLECTION QUESTIONS

1. Are you an extrovert or an introvert? Are you a visionary or a more detailed person who lives in the present of each day? Do you like structure, or do you prefer to just "see what happens"? Do your feelings influence your decisions more than your thoughts?

2. Can you identify these personality preferences in one or two of your closest friends? If so, what are they?

3. How do you deal with personality differences in your friendships? Do these differences cause conflict? Do you secretly get annoyed? Do you avoid talking about differences?

4. How would your friendships grow if you began trying to understand how the differences between you could be valuable to the friendship? How would this new vision change the purpose of your friendships?

*T*HE GROWN-UP FRIEND CONNECTS BY COMMUNICATING

[Erin]

Be truthful with your friend.
Truth and love are themselves friends;
one without the other makes each less.
FRIENDSHIP THERAPY

Listen gently to each other's sobs; your heart will
know abundant life. Listen gleefully to each other's
laughter; your hearts will know abundant joy.
FRIENDSHIP THERAPY

My dear brothers, take note of this:
Everyone should be quick to listen,
slow to speak and slow to become angry.
JAMES 1:19

Call to me and I will answer you and tell you great
and unsearchable things you do not know.
JEREMIAH 33:3

God designed us as relational beings who hunger for intimacy and deep connection. It is one of the most basic yearnings of the human heart. And that's why few things in life feel better than connecting with another person. That's also why we feel the sting so deeply when we are trying to connect with a friend and are not successful. To borrow a good friend's quote: Life is relationships; the rest is just details.

If we have this innate desire to connect deeply with another person—especially with our female friends—the question is, *How* do we connect?

Communication is how women typically connect. Men typically connect by doing things together or "hanging out." In other words, men experience intimacy through shared activities, and women experience intimacy through verbal self-disclosure and shared emotion.[1] This is why we don't normally see women on the ground wrestling, at a pickup game of basketball, or taking off together on a fishing trip. It's not that we don't enjoy those things or do them; it's just that we prefer to connect heart to heart. The bottom line is that God gave us not only a desire to connect relationally but also a yearning to achieve that connection through deep conversations in which we share our most intimate thoughts and feelings.

One of women's greatest strengths—talking—is also one of our greatest weaknesses. Without a doubt, the evil one has corrupted something that God intended as a blessing. Certainly because of the Fall, communication between friends can be one of the most frustrating and potentially damaging dynamics in a friendship. How many times have you felt . . .

deeply wounded by malicious gossip
overwhelmed by the intensity of someone's emotions
misunderstood after you shared your feelings
manipulated to do something a friend wanted
criticized for something you did
invalidated as you expressed your feelings
misrepresented to one friend by another
shut out by someone who stuffs her emotions
helpless as a friend formed negative beliefs about you

judged for how you feel or what you believe

minimized by someone who disagreed with something you
    shared

stonewalled by a friend who refused to confront you when
    hurt

hurt by a jealous friend who felt you were aggressively
    pursuing her friend

attacked by an explosive friend

frustrated when your friend didn't listen but instead offered
    advice or lectures

Unless you live on a deserted island like Tom Hanks in the movie *Cast Away*, you've experienced many if not all of these feelings and situations. I recently came to understand the power of gossip in a deeply personal way.

My son, Garrison, loves to tell a good story. Usually it is quite cute, since he is only four years old. He loves to give "dissertations" on various subjects. They can go on for up to forty-five minutes at times. I am sure he gets that from my husband's side of the family!

One time, however, Garrison's story wasn't so cute and actually caused quite a stir for my new friend, LeAnn. We had just put a contract on a new home in a close-knit community in Arkansas. My son was spending the day with LeAnn and her four-year-old son, Joshua, in our new neighborhood. As the two boys were playing on a swing set, Garrison began telling LeAnn one of his stories—a wild tale involving our family!

When I arrived to pick up Garrison from LeAnn's house, she looked a bit disturbed and had a few serious questions for me.

"I don't mean to pry," she asked reluctantly, "but were you married before?"

"What?"

"Have you been married before?" she asked again.

"No," I said. "Been with the same guy for fourteen years."

"Are you sure?" she continued. "Is there anyone you were *with* before who is now serving time?"

Serving time? I thought. *What on earth is she talking about?* I was dumbfounded. LeAnn seemed really sweet and all, so why would she possibly be asking me if I'd been married to a felon?

As I would soon find out, there was more behind her questioning than I knew. Apparently Garrison had "enlightened" LeAnn about our life prior to moving to Siloam Springs. The only problem was that his narrative was completely fictional! Garrison's story went something like this: "I am so happy that I have a new daddy. My old daddy was really mean and he went to jail after he choked me and hurt my sisters. My new daddy's name is Greg and he is nice. I am so glad my old daddy went to jail so I could have a new daddy!"

Out of the mouth of babes! Thanks to Garrison, this was one of the first impressions my new friend had of our family. And unfortunately, the story spread. Later, a friend told me that someone in the community asked her if I had previously been married to someone who is now in jail. Wonderful!

Of course, none of Garrison's story is remotely true, and I still don't know where his story actually came from. I have a sneaking suspicion that it probably has something to do with Greg, but I can't prove it! (But at least a creative mind is a sign of high intelligence, isn't it?)

While most of us can't spin a yarn as creatively as Garrison can, we've all been on the giving or receiving end of hurtful comments. Often our intentions are good, or we believe we are just being truthful. But the bottom line is that our mouths are powerful things. They can be used to lift someone up or bring her down.

> *The tongue is a small thing, but what enormous*
> *damage it can do. A great forest can be set on fire by*

one tiny spark. And the tongue is a flame of fire. It is full of wickedness, and poisons every part of the body . . . and can turn our whole lives into a blazing flame of destruction and disaster. JAMES 3:5-6, TLB

The tongue has the power of life and death, and those who love it will eat its fruit. PROVERBS 18:21

It is important to realize that our tongues have the power of life and death. It is unbelievable to me that the same muscle in a body is able to both bless and curse others—sometimes in the same breath. When we bless others with our words, we breathe life into them. However, when we curse someone, we "emotionally" take life from her.

Being hurt by others' words and hurting others with our words is part of engaging in relationships. I have been on the receiving end of others' cuts and jabs; however, I am also acutely aware of my own repeated failures. I have worked desperately and prayed ferociously to train my tongue to be disciplined in speech. As Garrison proved the day he told his tale, we don't always intend to hurt others, nor do we plan on getting our feelings hurt by others' words. It just happens. However, we have several choices:

- Are we willing to take responsibility for our words and learn methods to clean up our messes?
- Are we willing to be committed to seeking Christ's discernment about if and when we need to communicate our pain to others?
- When others fail us, are we willing to choose to forgive and begin the journey of healing our hearts? (See chapter 8 for more on forgiveness and chapter 4 on the importance of healing our hearts.)

- As grown-up friends, are we willing to make the choice to learn adult communication skills and not stick to the methods we learned from our families or in junior high school?

So how do we assess whether our current communication skills are working well and learn new and improved ways of interacting with others?

Let's begin by understanding something that has dramatically changed the way I communicate with my friends. As a matter of fact, if the following question can't be answered affirmatively, people will most likely have little or no desire to open up to you.

ARE YOU A SAFE FRIEND?

No doubt all of us have experienced feeling unsafe within a relationship at some point. I think of a phone conversation I had many years ago.

It was a weekday evening, and my husband, Greg, was out of town for the fourth time within a short period. I was pretty worn out from having him gone and was wishing he were home. I don't know about your household, but mine tends to be crazy around the dinner hour during weekdays—especially with Daddy gone!

The phone rang, and I saw on caller ID that it was my dear friend Kate. I was excited to hear from her since we hadn't had our usual daily conversation. So in the midst of my chaos, I chose to pick up the phone with the intention of saying, "I'll call you back!"

Well, things didn't quite end up going like I planned.

"Hey, Kate, what's going on?"

"Not a whole lot," she said. "I've been pretty busy today."

"Yeah, me too. . . . Greg's gone again and I am just worn out. I wish he weren't traveling so much right now."

"Really?" Kate snapped. After a short pause, she said, "Erin . . . why do you have such a hard time when your husband is gone? What is so hard about having him gone? I just don't understand."

I was speechless for a moment. (Talk about my buttons getting pushed!) "You know, I probably need to go," I finally said.

As I hung up the phone, I stood in my kitchen on the verge of tears, looking around at the unfolded laundry, the half-made dinner, and the kids' homework spread out all over the table. Not to mention that the children needed to be bathed. The hardest part was the loneliness I felt because I knew I had to do it all.

I then started to do what I typically do after an interaction like that—I started to beat myself up. I remember thinking, *Yeah, Erin, why can't you just do it all? Why can't you just pull it off alone? What's wrong with you?* This train of thinking obviously led me nowhere positive. Although Kate's words hurt, it actually was far more painful when I picked up the emotional stick and beat myself with it.

Talk about feeling unsafe.

If you are like Carrie and me, you long for friendships in which you feel completely safe. You want to feel free to open up and reveal who you really are and know that your friend will still love, accept, and value you—no matter what.

Yet many of us struggle with various aspects of intimacy because it requires openness, and openness makes us instantly vulnerable. We're not quite sure what a friend will say or do or how she'll use what she has learned about us. This is why a lack of desire to connect—or an avoidance of intimacy in general—usually has a lot to do with wanting to avoid being hurt, humiliated, or just plain uncomfortable.

As a way to lessen the risks, some of us develop strategies to connect without getting hurt. Some women spend much of their energy trying to hide. Others put up walls and try to project an image they think people will accept. Still others keep parts of themselves closed and protected. Then there are those who ignore or deny how they actually feel. Do you have any friends who get angry or demanding as a way of distracting others from their own vulnerability? The bottom line is that we may use a whole host of behaviors to try to avoid relational risks. Unfortunately, these strategies usually limit the level of intimacy in our friendships because it's hard for others to get close to us if we're standing on the other side of a thick wall or hiding behind a false mask.

In spite of the risks, the potential benefits of a close friendship are many. Intimacy creates the ideal opportunity to love deeply and be loved, experience a significant sense of belonging, have a clear sense of purpose in life, make a major difference in another's life, and fully express the best of who we are.

In order for intimacy and deep connection to occur, hearts must be open. Therefore, women typically try to achieve intimacy and deep connection by being more open or finding ways to create intimacy. For a moment, think of all the ways you try to create intimacy in your friendships. You probably spend hours talking and sharing your feelings. You may learn about each other's love languages and emotional needs. You talk on the phone and write e-mails. Perhaps you attend Bible study, eat lunch, play Bunco, shop at the mall, exercise, or work together. And the list goes on.

While on some level these shared activities do draw us together, they are actually unnecessarily difficult strategies since they don't alleviate our fears about the dangers of emotional vulnerability. Instead, the key is to focus significant time, attention, and energy into creating an environment that feels *safe.* We're not talking about physical safety. We're talking about emotional safety—feeling secure enough to truly open up and be known at a deep, intimate level.

The foundation of great communication—of great relationships, for that matter—is a truly safe environment, one that is safe physically, intellectually, spiritually, and emotionally. Remember, we are by nature inclined to want to be open and connect. Thus, openness can be understood as the default setting for human beings. No state of being takes less energy to maintain than openness, which involves being ourselves and just relaxing. Maintaining defenses, walls, and fortresses takes tremendous energy. Trying to get our friends to see us a certain way, whether by projecting an acceptable image or coming up with ways to get them to like or accept us, requires significant energy.

Before we talk about how to make our relationships safe, let's look at some typical things we do that can make friendships unsafe.

HOW WE MAKE A FRIENDSHIP UNSAFE
One of the surest elements that will make a relationship feel unsafe is gossip!

I've had to work on myself in this area as much as anyone else. First and foremost, I have learned that if we are going to look at what is coming out of our mouths, we must first look at our own hearts. Do you believe that what seeps out of our mouths indicates what is in our hearts? Luke 6:45 confirms this:

> *The good man brings good things out of the good stored up in his heart, and the evil man brings evil things out of the evil stored up in his heart. For out of the overflow of his heart his mouth speaks.*

There was a season in my life years ago when there were many ugly things coming out of my mouth. I was stunned at some of the things I would find myself saying—even about family and friends whom I dearly loved.

One incident that taught me the impact of gossip is still crystal clear in my mind—though it happened more than fifteen years ago. I was a sophomore in high school, and I hung out with quite a few seniors because my best friend, Inger, was a senior.

We often hung around with a group of guys—who were strictly our friends. One night when we were together, someone mentioned that a girl named Kim liked one of our guy friends, Steve.

Even though it is hard for me to remember exactly what I said after that conversation, I *may* have repeated it to my older brother when I got home that night. I think I was in such shock over the confrontation the next day that it's hard to remember the exact details.

I was walking out of biology class toward my locker when I bumped into Kim. She didn't look very happy—and I soon realized that I was the source of her unhappiness.

Suddenly Kim grabbed me by the arms and slammed me against the lockers. I was in shock as pain shot throughout my body.

Kim then got very close to my face and glared at me. "I heard *you* told everyone that I like Steve!" she spurted out.

"I promise that it wasn't me," I shot back, even though I really didn't remember what I had said and didn't think it was that big of a deal anyway.

Apparently I was wrong, because once Kim eased her grip, I began to realize that even though I hadn't intended to harm her with my words, I had.

My brother later told me that when they were all in drama

class someone began chanting the news of Kim's crush on Steve. At some point after all the brutal teasing, she asked who was responsible for this false rumor. My name came up. Figures!

Although I really don't think I started the rumor—I originally had heard it from someone else—I was left with the consequences. Ouch, my back hurts when I think about it!

The fear I felt that day has remained with me for a long time, and I will never forget the look in Kim's eyes. She was hurt, and in her mind I was to blame. It was a hard lesson, but every time we carelessly repeat something we've heard about another person, we are gossiping. You'd think this experience would have cured me from ever gossiping again, but unfortunately, like many women, at times I still fail in this area. Just like in high school, I don't usually intend to harm someone by repeating something I've heard, but the bottom line is this—it's gossip. Proverbs 11:13 says, "A gossip betrays a confidence, but a trustworthy man keeps a secret." With God's help and grace, I continue to seek His discernment on when to speak and when not to. Only through Him can we win this battle.

Controlling our mouths will be a constant, intentional battle for many of us for the rest of our lives. As relational beings, we women long for connection with other women. And unfortunately, gossiping about someone often provides that connecting point. Carrie and I define gossip as "spreading intimate or private rumors, or facts of a personal, sensational, or intimate nature about someone else who is not part of the conversation (either spoken or written)." In other words, when we share information with someone who is not part of the problem or solution or when we break our friend's trust by sharing her private information, we are gossiping.

One recent research study found that 65 percent of what

people talk about in their social conversations could be categorized as gossip. They also reported that this finding did not vary much according to age or gender.[2] Marion Underwood, a social psychologist at the University of Texas at Dallas, says that gossip really "walks the line between what is acceptable and what is not. It is completely unacceptable for me to punch my colleague, but if I tell people he drinks too much, I am less likely to be called out on it."[3] Let's face it: It is much easier to talk about someone behind her back than to speak the words directly to her. We don't have to face our fear of confrontation.

Sociologists have called gossip a "social weapon," a harmful tool that some will use against others. With nicknames such as "gossip hounds" that are given to those who gossip, it is obvious that gossip and its effects carry a strong negative influence. When we suspect our conversation may be crossing the line into gossip, we need to ask ourselves: Is the information something negative about a third party who isn't there to defend herself? Does passing on this information make us feel that we are better than the person we are talking about? Are we using the information that we are passing along to better our own appearance in some way?

While we often gossip with a friend in an attempt to draw closer to her, what's interesting is that the opposite is likely to occur instead. After all, if we're willing to talk about someone else when she's not around, our friend may wonder what we say about her when she's absent. As Blaise Pascal, a seventeenth-century philosopher, said, "I maintain that, if everyone knew what others said about him, there would not be four friends in the world."

Gossip can poison our perceptions of another person. As Proverbs 26:22 says, "The words of a gossip are like choice morsels; they go down to a man's inmost parts." When we talk negatively about someone, those listening may begin to resent that person.

As he was growing up, my husband, Greg, heard countless stories about his uncle Ronnie from my father-in-law. When they were boys, Ronnie would pick on Greg's father, teasing him and committing various other dastardly deeds. As you can imagine, the first time Greg met his uncle Ronnie when he was about five, the reception wasn't as positive as Ronnie had probably envisioned. After the two brothers warmly embraced, Greg's father introduced him. As his uncle affectionately extended his arms to greet his nephew, Greg walked up, looked him right in the eyes, shouted, "This is for my daddy!" and punched Ronnie squarely in the gut. Vengeance was his! Interestingly, Greg and Uncle Ronnie were never that close.

The bottom line is that gossip erodes the foundation of safety in a friendship. But why? What is the real consequence of gossip? It often leads to negative thinking about someone else. That alone makes a friendship feel unsafe.

GOSSIP'S DEADLY IMPACT

When I was about to turn nineteen, I was in hot pursuit of my dream car. I dreamed about owning a black Suzuki Samurai— I wanted one so desperately. However, I soon began to notice that everyone else in Phoenix, Arizona, seemed to be driving a black Suzuki Samurai. I was shocked! Why was it suddenly the most driven car? I had never noticed so many before!

Negative beliefs work just like that: When you begin to believe something about someone or are looking for something specific in her behavior, you will find overwhelming evidence of what you are looking for. Just like the car incident—I was looking for Samurais and suddenly they were everywhere!

Gossip often triggers these negative beliefs, or at least exacerbates them. Negative thinking is powerful because the way we perceive and interpret others' behavior has a direct impact on our relationships. If we look for and believe negative things about our friends' behavior, we will find them. And guess what? This will negatively impact the friendship. We will suddenly be overwhelmed with the sheer number of negative behaviors we see in our friends. This can also be true with a spouse, family members, coworkers, and even children.

Confirmation bias is a fancy psychological term that describes negative thinking even better. Basically, this term is defined like this: You will find evidence of what you believe about another person (positive or negative) in everything he or she says or does. Romans 14:14 supports this idea: "To him who thinks anything to be unclean, to him it is unclean" (NASB).

As you begin to look for or notice negative behaviors in your friend, the way you treat your friend is affected. In other words, we have a tendency to treat others in accordance with what we think or believe about them. As a result, our friend usually begins to behave in a way consistent with our expectations. People tend to live up to or down to our beliefs about them.

Once negative thinking and beliefs invade a friendship, they produce an unsafe environment, which leads to a spirit of hopelessness and demoralization. Ultimately, this ends up leaving little hope for the overall friendship. Can you think of any of your friends who gradually drifted away? Your friendship may have gotten off to a great start, but over the months you began assuming negative things about your friend. Suddenly you noticed your friend behaving in cruel, unloving ways. You may have heard things about your friend (gossip) that added fuel to the negative beliefs you had about her. Next the friendship began to cool, and before you knew it the friend was pretty much out of your life. You wondered what in the world had happened. Often, though not always, such broken friendships are the result of negative thinking.

We encourage you to go back and evaluate whether any negative beliefs invaded your relationship. Did you fall into the trap of viewing your friend through dark lenses? If so, how can you prevent this from happening again?

Besides gossip and negative beliefs, many other attitudes and actions can make a friendship feel unsafe. How many of these attitudes have wounded you—or have you used to hurt others?

1. *Criticism or critical attitude:* We judge our friend with a hurtful attitude.
2. *Competitiveness:* We spend our time comparing ourselves to what our friend has or does, and we work to keep up with her.
3. *Blaming:* We are unaware what goes on inside of us emotionally when interacting with others, so we react and blame our friend for our emotional state.
4. *Manipulation:* We work to get something we want or to impress others without being up front about our motives.
5. *Unwillingness to confront:* We avoid being open with our friend about how we truly feel or how we've been hurt.
6. *Jealousy:* We are unable to celebrate our friend's successes and joys.
7. *High level of emotion:* We say exactly what we feel without considering the effects on others; in other words, we have difficulty determining where to draw the line with sharing (oversharing).
8. *Complex dynamics within groups of women:* We jockey for position within a group of friends. The focus is on us and how we feel or what we can get out of the friendship, not on how we can improve the relationships themselves.
9. *The need to talk instead of listening:* We give advice instead of listening. As a result, we end up misunderstanding our friend's real feelings or her situation.

HOW TO MAKE A FRIENDSHIP SAFE

Let us say it again: *When friends feel safe, they are naturally inclined to open their hearts.* Intimacy occurs effortlessly and naturally when hearts open to one another, because that state of openness requires less energy to maintain. Safety will help you create a climate in which you can build open friendships that will grow and flourish. It will help you build relationships in which you and the other woman will feel cherished, honored, and alive. It's almost as if this sets a soothing tone that will allow you to feel relaxed in your friendships.

The good news is that you can create an open atmosphere in your friendships that will allow both people to be their true selves. But the focus must be on creating *safety*.

In your quest to have the "best of the best" in your life and relationships, make creating safety in your friendships a top priority. Start this process by answering some basic questions:

1. How safe are your relationships for you and your friends (using a scale of 0–10, with 10 being the most safe)?
2. In what ways have you made your relationships unsafe for your friends?
3. What do you do in response to feeling unsafe?
4. What would cause you to feel safe when sharing your deepest need or hurt with a friend?

Having a foundation of safety—especially emotional safety—makes opening up significantly easier. When you and your friend know that both of you are committed to creating a safe relationship, you avoid things that would cause hurt in either of you, and you begin building a foundation for a great friendship. Ideally, your relationship should feel like one of the safest places on earth.

My friend Mary is wonderful at creating this environment. It causes my heart to remain open and free to share with her my thoughts, feelings, and concerns. She is a great listener, she is quick to give compliments, and she is committed to learn through her relational trials. She will also on occasion call and say, "Hey, I had no business telling you about my friend. Will you forgive me?" All these behaviors cause me to feel safe. And guess what? She is the first person I want to talk to when I have an issue or need someone to listen. I know that she is human and might not always be perfect at creating a safe environment, but I have seen her own her faults and seek to repair the damage. However, I have been in other relationships that have reminded me of trying to connect with a porcupine! It doesn't feel safe, and my heart ends up closing.

What does a "porcupine" friend feel like? Such a friend might disagree with every word you say, invalidate every feeling you have, continually try to overtake the conversation, or maybe even hurl accusations at you. It just doesn't feel good, and it definitely does not feel safe!

I encourage you again to take inventory. Do you create an environment in which you'd want to open up if you were your friend? We can *all* behave like porcupines at times; however, is this your general stance when someone is trying to share her heart with you? Do you immediately become defensive, or do you allow her to share her struggle? Ask yourself, *What is it like to communicate with me?*

I would never suggest you open your heart in an environment that does not feel safe to you. It is important to develop discernment—sensing an environment's warmth and safety level. If you have a basket number one friend who is often a "porcupine," it may be time to sit down and have a talk about how this impacts you and your relationship, or you may even need to make a "basket shift."

I encourage you to consider two things. First, pray and seek the Lord's discernment on how to handle this situation. Second, handle your friend's heart with care. Be a model of how to treat others. Treat her with the same care and tenderness with which you would like to be treated.

Jesus is the perfect model of this. "'He committed no sin, and no deceit was found in his mouth.' When they hurled their insults at him, he did not retaliate; when he suffered, he made no threats" (1 Peter 2:22-23). Thank goodness He gives us grace—sometimes minute by minute and other times day by day.

As we embark on this journey together, let's adopt the attitude of becoming lifelong learners of Christ. He calls us to become more like Him every day, which includes reflecting His graciousness in our speech. Commit with us today to seek Him for a true and perfect model of what we should strive for in our speech. Call on Him for His strength and guidance throughout this process—the process of retraining and relearning how to communicate as grown-up friends.

Safety paves the way for great communication to take place. When your friend feels safe, her heart will open and intimacy can flourish. Here are a few things you can do to make your relationships safe for your friends:

1. *Honor each other:* Recognize your friend's value. (See Romans 12:10.)
2. *Recognize when your fear buttons have been pushed:* Manage your own emotions with the Lord's guidance. This will prevent you from reacting instead of thinking through your responses.
3. *Be willing to seek forgiveness:* Why are the four simple words "Will you forgive me?" so difficult to get out sometimes? The root is often pride and an unwillingness to admit that we are not perfect.

4. *Speak life into your friends:* Be willing to tell your friend when you see something positive in her life or the potential you see in her.

5. *Avoid escalation (screaming, yelling, threats, etc.):* These behaviors destroy safety within any relationship.

6. *Create ground rules for both participants to follow:* These lay out acceptable behaviors and unacceptable behaviors. They create limits and nets to protect the relationship from being harmed.

By the way, you can apply these principles when you're with a group of friends too. For instance, if one friend is encouraging you to exclude another simply because she wants you to herself, recognize her demand as destructive and unhealthy. Being grown up means learning to recognize unhealthy behaviors in ourselves and refusing to go along with another friend who is engaging in them.

Once the relationship feels safe, you can apply communication skills to be a grown-up communicator. So, exactly how does a grown-up communicate?

1. **A grown-up friend is willing to confront.** Confrontation is not easy! It is something that I have tried to avoid at all costs. But I can tell you from experience that this has gotten me nowhere. It has forfeited many opportunities for growth in my relationships. It has also on occasion ended up destroying a friendship. Matthew 18:15-16 speaks about what the Lord calls us to do in our relationships: "If your brother sins against you, go and show him his fault, just between the two of you. If he listens to you, you have won your brother over. But if he will not listen, take one or two others along, so that 'every matter may be established by the testimony of two or three witnesses.'"

Clearly we are called to go to our sister when we have been wronged. However, how do we determine if we truly have been sinned against? To do this, we must be willing to keep short accounts with others. In other words, if we feel we have been wronged, we must be willing to go to another and try to explain what we are experiencing or feeling. However, before going to her, we must first deal with ourselves, which means identifying the buttons that have been pushed, our reactions, and our feelings. By working through these issues with the Lord's help, we can go to our friend with open hearts . . . which leaves us in a less emotionally explosive state and more likely to see a positive outcome.

What's the alternative? If we go to our friend with closed hearts and possibly blaming spirits, we end up insisting she make our feelings better. Obviously, that is much less likely to lead to a positive solution.

The Lord has given me many opportunities to learn more about this matter. Sometimes I have really failed the test; other times I have done better. Sometimes I honestly believed that the issue would just go away if I ignored it. Other times I feared the reaction I would receive, or I feared making an enemy. Les and Leslie Parrott, in their book *A Good Friend*, offer some wise counsel: "Speak the truth, because if you are afraid of making enemies you'll never have good friends."[4]

Confrontation does put you in a risky position; however, with the Lord guiding you and caring for you during the ups and downs of your relationships, it is worth the risk.

When you are faced with a challenging issue in a friendship, turn to the Lord! In their book *The Power of a Positive Friend,* Karol Ladd and Terry Ann Kelly offer some good suggestions on seeking the Lord's guidance before talking with a friend about difficult issues:[5]

- Ask Him to reveal the truth about your heart (see Psalm 139:23-24).
- Become aware of the plank in your own eye (see Luke 6:39-42).
- Ask Him for discernment on how to handle the situation (see 2 Timothy 3:16-17).
- Approach your friend with humility (see Luke 18:10-14).
- Pray for your friend to be open to your concerns (see Hebrews 10:25).
- Use the "sandwich approach"—offering a positive about your friend or the situation, then your concern, and then another positive or affirmation (see 1 Corinthians 4:21).

Last, ask the Lord for guidance about the best time and approach for sharing your concern with a friend. When possible, the best approach is a face-to-face meeting, since your friend will be able to pick up on your nonverbal cues (facial expressions, hand gestures, body posture) as well as your words. (After all, these nonverbal cues account for the majority of what is actually communicated.) Phone calls and e-mails don't allow nonverbal communication, which decreases the chances of a positive outcome.

Of course, e-mail looks like an easy and convenient way to tackle your relationship issues. Yet I've noticed some definite drawbacks. Recently, I received an e-mail from my friend Susan that really upset me. I couldn't understand why my usually supportive friend was e-mailing me, encouraging me to get over my hurt

feelings of a devastating situation that my husband and
I had been part of. I truly was hurt. Since she was not
in town, I decided not to return the e-mail and placed a
phone call to her to discuss the situation. Susan laughed
out loud when I told her my interpretation of the e-
mail. I had completely missed the meaning of what she
was communicating. I couldn't believe I had gotten it so
backward. I fail every now and then, but I really try to
avoid e-mail for anything but positive affirmations and
information exchanges within my relationships.

2. **A grown-up friend is a great listener.** "Be quick to listen,
slow to speak and slow to become angry" (James 1:19).
After reading this verse years ago, I began to wonder
what our world would be like if everyone adopted James
1:19 as her goal in communicating. Can you imagine?
Everyone would want to first listen and then respond
slowly and thoughtfully. Angry outbursts would be
history.

Okay, maybe that isn't totally realistic, but what a
great foundation to adopt and strive to put to work in
our relationships. I know that when someone honors
me by listening to my heart, I desire to do the same in
return. Good communication happens when we choose to
make our primary goal understanding rather than being
understood.

Listening is defined this way: "to make an effort to
hear; to pay attention, as to warning or advice."[6] Listening really means that when another person is speaking,
we are not thinking about what we are going to say when
she stops talking. Listening is choosing to be and remain
present.

Think about how often you have been with a friend

who appeared to be listening, but intuitively you could tell she was thinking about something else. Maybe she was planning what she would say next. Or maybe she was thinking about what she was going to have for lunch later.

I often catch myself doing this exact thing. Sometimes when I am writing or reading an e-mail, the phone will ring. Instead of stopping what I've been working on, I attempt to do both (now I've done it—I've revealed my secret!). Obviously, I fail every time at truly being the listener I desire to be. Listening requires giving undivided attention. If you're the mother of small children, I am sure you have grown quite used to talking over smaller voices or crying. That's why I encourage you to make some "kid-free" time with your friends—especially when you need to discuss sensitive or heated topics.

The following are some helpful ways to be a great listener:

Be empathetic. Put yourself in your friend's shoes. Have you ever experienced what she is going through? What would it be like to be in her situation? It's irrelevant whether your friend's feelings are logical or illogical. The goal is to care about her feelings and her heart. The purpose is not so much for you to understand; it's for you to help her feel understood and cared for. This is true empathy. On the other hand, think of the many ways we communicate that we don't care how people feel.

- "Why do you get so emotional?"
- "Your emotions are out of control."
- "That's not how you really feel!"

Don't go to the other extreme either. Caring for your friend's heart does not equal:

- resolving or "fixing" the issue
- having to agree with everything she says or how she feels
- being responsible for her feelings
- making changes
- always admitting guilt or fault, or apologizing

Instead, caring means:

- Replacing judgment with curiosity. Instead of judging her for feeling a certain way, be curious about *why* she feels the way she does. Also, instead of assuming you already understand a situation, be open to finding out more.
- Allowing yourself to feel someone else's pain. In other words, let your heart be touched by your friend's emotions and feelings.
- Not taking responsibility for her reaction. Sometimes we hope a person will respond to us in a particular way or do something as a result of our caring. Since we have no control over what someone does with our caring, our responsibility is to be kind. We always have the option to say something like, "I remember how tired I was when I went through the teenage years with my oldest daughter. I was worn out from all the daily discussions and disagreements we had about her curfew."

Summarize what was said. Look for the emotional message of what your friend is communicating. For example, say, "If I understood you right, it sounds like you are having a difficult time with your teenage daughter. You are feeling hopeless, frustrated, and uncertain about what to do next."

Ask open-ended questions or make open-ended statements that lead to deeper sharing, such as "Tell me what you are struggling with most."

Offer validation of your friend's feelings—even if you don't totally agree with them. Feelings are not right or wrong. They just are. Often someone else's feelings won't make sense to us, but that shouldn't keep us from acknowledging and validating her feelings.

- "I can understand how you would feel frustrated with your daughter when she hasn't been following the curfew rules you set with her."

Be compassionate to a friend who is down.

- "I can't imagine how taxing this has been on you. Can I do anything to help you out?"

3. **A grown-up friend is aware of negative beliefs and gives her friends the benefit of the doubt.** The word *fight* is an exact descriptor of what the grown-up friend needs to do in order to decrease the devastating impact negative beliefs have on any relationship. Early in our marriage, Greg and I had to battle some negative beliefs another couple had formed about us. They chose to misinterpret the reasons behind a decision we had made but never came to us to ask us to explain our desires and intentions. It was heart-wrenching to watch our friends begin believing that they did not truly know us after several years of friendship. The negative beliefs overtook their minds, and suddenly they saw us in a different light. It was painful to be

on the receiving end of this, and sadly enough the friendship ended, partly due to negative beliefs. This taught us a serious lesson: We must choose to fight these thoughts. The following four suggestions, which Greg outlined in *The Marriage You've Always Dreamed Of,* can be helpful in this process:[7]

Step 1: Develop an "I could be wrong" attitude toward others. Paul encouraged Christians to be mature in their thinking: "Do not be children in your thinking; yet in evil be infants, but in your thinking be mature" (1 Corinthians 14:20, NASB). Mature thinking acknowledges that we can *never* be 100 percent accurate in our interpretation of our friends' thoughts, words, and behaviors. Thus, we must adapt a humble attitude—one that is tentative about the accuracy of our conclusions.

Step 2: Substitute more reasonable responses for the negative thought. This has had a substantial impact on my friendships. At one point in my life, I truly believed that my perceptions were 100 percent accurate. Once I was humbled in my thinking, I begin to realize that I could draw other conclusions—often more positive ones—about what my friend had done or said. I learned that this had a dramatically positive impact on my thinking and thus the overall friendship.

Step 3: Check out the accuracy of your negative thinking. Once we consider alternative explanations for what our friend did—since we still do not know the truth—we need to ask for her input. This may get your heart racing, as it does mine, because this will lead to a conversation that may feel uncomfortable—maybe even like a confrontation. Yet all you're really doing is asking for your friend's insight on the situation. It truly doesn't have to be confrontational at all. It is not about what you are saying—it is how you choose to say it. Try starting the conversation with "I have noticed _____. Can you help me understand this?"

Step 4: Keep track of positive behavior. When we make a point of watching for our friend's positive actions and letting her know what we've seen, those negative beliefs are likely to be replaced by positive ones. Scripture itself encourages us to dwell on what is good: "Whatever is true, whatever is honorable, whatever is right, whatever is pure, whatever is lovely, whatever is of good repute, if there is any excellence and if anything worthy of praise, let your mind dwell on these things" (Philippians 4:8, NASB).

One of the best ways to care for your friendships, especially basket number one relationships, is to guard them from becoming infected with negative thinking. Women are typically perceivers, which means our perceptions can really drive our feelings. That's why it is important to acknowledge that your perceptions might be wrong. Give your friend the benefit of the doubt until you can visit with her (not someone else) to discuss your concerns. These steps alone will cause you to be a better, more positive communicator.

4. **A grown-up friend adopts a "loyalty to the absent" attitude.** "Mommy," young Billy asked his mother on the way to school, "where are all the idiots?"

"What!" his mother said in disbelief. "Why on earth are you asking me that?"

Confused by his mother's reaction, young Billy answered, "Yesterday when Daddy took me to school we saw five idiots along the way."

What do you say about others in front of your friends? Is it positive or negative? Is it uplifting, or does it leave them with a bitter taste in their mouths? Now I don't go around calling people idiots or swearing like a sailor. That's not my style. However, I *have* made sarcastic comments and gossiped to a friend now and then.

Paul's words in James 3:5-6 are so true: "The tongue is a small part of the body, but it makes great boasts. Consider what a great forest is set on fire by a small spark. The tongue also is a fire, a world of evil among the parts of the body. It corrupts the whole person, sets the whole course of his life on fire, and is itself set on fire by hell."

Our goal should be loyalty to the absent. In other words, we should strive to honor others with our words (tongues) when they are not present. This creates trust and confidence. If your friend doesn't hear you gossiping about others, she will not wonder what you are saying about her when she is gone. "Through the blessing of the upright a city is exalted, but by the mouth of the wicked it is destroyed" (Proverbs 11:11).

5. **A grown-up friend takes personal responsibility.** Ultimately, as grown-up friends we are responsible for the choices we make in communicating within our friendships. We shouldn't blame or point fingers at others for our circumstances or feelings. It can be difficult, in moments of intense conversations, but ultimately we must *choose* what we believe about our friends, what we will do about it, and ultimately how we will communicate any concerns to our friend.

To do this well, we must turn to the Lord and ask Him for His mind and understanding. We can choose to set our minds on things of the flesh or on things of the Spirit.

Ultimately, this will determine what we communicate. Romans 8:5-8 says it well: "Those who are according to the flesh set their minds on the things of the flesh, but those who are according to the Spirit, the things of the Spirit. For the mind set on the flesh is death, but the mind set on the Spirit is life and peace, because the mind set on the flesh is hostile toward God; for it does not subject itself to the law of God, for it is not even able to do so; and those who are in the flesh cannot please God" (NASB).

As I journey toward becoming more grown up, I continue to seek the Lord's guidance in this area. Recently, Carrie and I had an opportunity to practice this principle. I inadvertently heard something she had said to someone concerning me. At first, I wasn't sure what to make of the comment "Erin is way too overcommitted." I knew that remark wasn't far from the truth, as I live at a very rapid pace and get a lot of energy from people and activities—still, "overcommitted"?

I prayed and knew that I needed to try to understand what Carrie meant by this and at the same time fight the ferocious negative beliefs roaring in my head. The next day Carrie called me, and I had the opportunity to gently mention that someone had told me what she had said.

Carrie said, "Well, I actually said that after I had listed ten positives about you, Erin. And my intention was to be protective of you and your busy schedule." My heart immediately opened and I was grateful that I had brought it up, as I could have gone down "the bunny trail," coming up with all kinds of possible meanings to her comment. Our conversation actually led me to feel even more safe in our friendship.

Learning to be responsible for what I believe about my friends and how I communicate with them has changed the fate of several relationships in my life. However, the only way this has been possible is through seeking the Lord and His mind. Will you join me in this journey of having healthier communication in our friendships?

The grown-up girlfriend . . .

. . . *knows the foundation of great communication is a truly safe environment.*

· ·

REFLECTION QUESTIONS

1. As women, one of our greatest strengths is talking; however, it is one of our greatest weaknesses, too. Do you struggle with gossip? Have you been wounded by someone who gossiped about you?

2. Think of a current relationship in your life that is not safe. List three things you can do to make that relationship safer.

8

THE GROWN-UP FRIEND FORGIVES

[Carrie]

Good friendships are fragile things and require as much care as any other fragile and precious thing.
RANDOLPH BOURNE

When your friend hurts you, your friendship can survive. Don't try to hide your pain. Talk about it and enjoy the delightful effervescence of reconciliation.
FRIENDSHIP THERAPY

The best way to get the last word is to apologize.[1]

I will never forget coming home a few years ago to find a letter from a friend in the mailbox. I'd instantly connected with this woman when my family first moved to Colorado many years before. I appreciated her spunk and her smile—as well as our common interest in golf. Our kids also got along well, so we often took care of one another's children. Since neither of us had family living nearby, we celebrated holidays and birthdays together. In addition, we attended the same church and Bible studies, and we met regularly at 6 a.m. to pray together. (I haven't gotten up that early to pray with anyone else since!) We now lived in different states and had not kept in close contact.

In the letter, this precious lady outlined some behavior she felt had been hurtful to me and our friendship. Then she asked for my forgiveness. I was stunned and touched. Before long, I felt motivated to respond to her letter, disclosing how I thought I'd contributed to the problem. I told her I looked forward to reestablishing our friendship, one that could honor and glorify God in new ways.

This is the forgiveness process, plain and simple. My friend and I are so thankful that we listened to the Holy Spirit on this one and that we resolved our differences before I was diagnosed with cancer. So often we wait to resolve our issues until crisis strikes.

The reality is that sooner or later in every relationship, someone's feelings will be hurt—whether or not that was the intention. Yet many times our attempts to resolve our differences do not go as beautifully and biblically as the process did between my friend and me. Unless we consciously choose to practice the communication skills Erin introduced in the last chapter—no matter how difficult that is—forgiveness may seem impossible. We can become so easily entwined in the conflict, arguing over who's right, who's wrong, who hurt whom the most. We focus on the behavior and sometimes never get to forgiveness, let alone restoration.

We know so little about the true process of forgiveness because so few of us complete it. Yet a friendship—especially an intimate basket one friendship—cannot survive without the ability to go through forgiveness. In this chapter we want to provide a biblical framework for understanding forgiveness and motivate you to forgive (or seek forgiveness) whenever God calls you to do so. A friendship will never be the same when true forgiveness is experienced: It will deepen and grow at levels never before experienced.

WHY FORGIVENESS?

Scripture tells us that forgiveness is the lifeline to salvation and eternity with God. Jesus died on the cross so we might be forgiven. Now He calls us to forgive just as He forgave (see Colossians 3:13). Forgiveness is not a light subject or an easy process. Often, because we have not experienced healthy, godly forgiveness, we give up on a broken relationship and never experience the fruit of mercy and of coming out on the other side of reconciliation. We are an impatient people living in a fast-food culture. Most of us want results now.

Although forgiving and seeking forgiveness is risky, if we choose not to do so, our relationships will not grow, and more hurt feelings are likely to develop. Pretty soon we have a mountain of hurt and pain to wade through. Forgiveness levels the mountain of hurt feelings, nurtures the heart, and encourages safety and intimacy. That is why we must choose to forgive and seek forgiveness.

THE BEGINNINGS OF FORGIVENESS

Many of us have heard sermons and read Scripture passages on the topic of forgiveness. Perhaps we have had some experience with it in relationships. Others would say that we don't know exactly what forgiveness is and definitely do not see it working in our relationships. We may even have a difficult time feeling forgiven by God.

I love Ephesians 4:32, which says, "Be kind and compassionate to one another, forgiving each other, just as in Christ God forgave you." Before we can forgive others, we must embrace God's forgiveness of our weaknesses and our sins. When we ask Him to forgive us—and we mean what we ask— He does forgive us. We must then believe it and begin to act on this truth.

It is the evil one who tells us things like, *Oh, you know you can't believe that; you have always messed up and you will continue to do so.* Don't believe him! Christ died for you and will continually offer you grace when you need to be forgiven. I so treasure the song "Untitled Hymn (Come to Jesus)," which is sung by Chris Rice. Talking about the inevitability of our sin, the song says, "Sometimes we fall . . . so fall on Jesus and live!"[2] Forgiveness and being forgiven are always about fresh life, strong and whole. The ability to forgive begins by recognizing that the Lord Jesus Christ forgave us first.

According to Dr. Everett Worthington, author of the *Handbook of Forgiveness*, forgiveness often begins with a decision to forgive, even when a person's emotions aren't in line with that decision.[3] This may be especially true when that person has experienced extreme hurt or betrayal. In other words, we can offer grace and compassion, even if we don't feel our friend deserves it. That is what Christ did for us on the cross. He did not deserve to die for our wrongdoings, yet He has the capacity to get inside our hearts and see the world from our eyes and have compassion on us. Christ did that frequently with those He dealt with, as in the example of the woman at the well. He knew her situation and He knew her heart even before she opened her mouth. He did not condemn her; He simply stated truth with love (see John 4:4-30). Just as Christ doesn't condemn us, we can offer understanding to our friend (see 1 John 3:19-20).

Worthington points out that one of the keys to forgiveness is coming to the point where we empathize with the one who has wronged us; that is, we learn to see the world from the other person's heart. We also realize we are just one step away from committing the wrong done to us. Through empathy, we can release hurt and anger and truly forgive.[4]

After all, that's what we desire from those we love, isn't it? That they would see the world from our hearts? Scripture tells us to gently restore those who've sinned, while remembering how easily we could fall into that same sin. We are all just one step away from committing the sin of those around us (see Galatians 6:1). Unless we believe and apply this Scripture, our pride and anger will often get the best of us.

When we don't forgive, we're often the ones who suffer most. A friend once preached a message on forgiveness. He told of an elderly woman who had been hurt by some family members and had carried that hurt all her life. She was unable to trust people with her heart and engage in relationships. This pain had turned into bitterness and anger, which led her to live a sad and lonely life. In fact, people were surprised to discover that this woman wasn't really elderly at all. She was actually twenty years younger than she looked!

When I heard this story, I was challenged to ask myself whether I was carrying anger, bitterness, or resentment that was leading to mistrust and isolation. I certainly didn't want to look twenty years older than I am! Who wants that? Seriously, pent-up anger and unforgiveness eventually catch up with us. We could be just like that bitter woman: negative and critical people whom nobody wants to be with—unless we learn to forgive.

FORGIVENESS IS NOT . . .

I enjoy harmony. I like my relationships to feel good, and I don't want to raise conflict if I don't have to. I have learned over the years, though, that the price of false harmony is too high.

At the same time, I know that forgiveness is not easy! It takes emotional and spiritual awareness. As a counselor, I have frequent opportunities to observe the process of forgiveness and have picked up a few lessons over the years. For instance, forgiveness doesn't usually follow a quick and easy "I am sorry" that doesn't acknowledge the hurtful behavior or allow the wronged person to process her emotion. Have you ever had someone say to you, "I said I was sorry, what more do you want!"?

Also, forgiveness does not always bring reconciliation. If we choose to forgive our friend but she continues her behavior or refuses to acknowledge the pain she's caused, reconciliation may not happen. Reconciliation often requires repentance or changed behavior. If a friend wrongs you and does not repent, meaning she doesn't name the offense and behave differently to avoid committing the same offense again, you must figure out what God would have you do. If the offense seems pretty severe, the friendship may be compromised or you may decide to move it to a different "basket." Do pray about the situation, perhaps even talking about it with a counselor or writing out your thoughts. You might even take the risk of telling your friend that her lack of repentance seems to be coming between you and her.

Forgiving our friend does not mean that we will automatically forget, especially when we have been deeply hurt. Our emotions take time to catch up to our heads. We also need time to rebuild our trust and love. We need Jesus for this emotional process. If our friend has repented and we've reconciled, with time the heart can catch up. It is so important not to keep "reminding" our friend of what she did. Time, good communication, and conflict skills can help us overcome the thoughts that may be plaguing us. The evil one works overtime to destroy all relationships. He hates vital, intimate relationships and knows that if we dwell on the way our friend has hurt us, our friendship can't flourish. Be aware of this reality.

HOW DO WE FORGIVE?

Some of us are particularly sensitive. We may get hurt ten times in one day! Our friend doesn't call us, she and her husband go to dinner with another couple, she signs up for Bible study without asking us to sign up too, her child has someone over to play and doesn't invite our child, and the list could go on. If we are getting hurt this often, the first thing to do is to look at ourselves. Part of the problem may be our possessiveness. Our friend will never be able to meet all our needs. (We talk more about this in the next chapter.) If we constantly feel slighted over small matters, we need to learn to overlook these unintended insults.

Since we find our identities as cherished children of God, we do not have to get our identities through someone else. We need to guard against personalization, the tendency to take another's words or actions personally and assume they were directed at us. Being too sensitive will make us miserable and create unneeded worry and anxiety. On the other hand, encouraging our friend in her choices and learning to make our own will soon make us less sensitive to unintended slights.

If we truly have been wronged, we cannot forgive until we have let go of our desire to get even or hurt the person back. We need to ask ourselves, *Am I willing to forgive? Can I look beyond my friend's behavior and give up the hurt it caused?* When we do, we may be surprised to find that the answer is no. Often we want payback. One reason you may not have thought of is this: Being sad or wounded drains us of energy, while anger gives us energy, which seems preferable. When we are mad, we want our friend to pay. We may actually enjoy the one-up position that some of us feel when we have been hurt. Forgiveness requires us to give that up! Anger is a secondary emotion, an emotion that follows another emotion, such as fear or hurt. Going back to the first emotion we felt allows us to give up the desire for revenge.

Second, whether our friend comes to talk to us about the offense or not, we need to learn to look at her with the eyes of our heavenly Father. After all, that is who is looking at us! The apostle Paul tells us to "be imitators of God, therefore, as dearly loved children and live a life of love, just as Christ loved us and gave himself up for us" (Ephesians 5:1-2). As we look at our friend with the same tenderness with which God looks at us, we'll come to want good for our friend, especially if she comes to us or is open to us coming to her with our wounds.

Third, expect forgiveness to take time. We can make a decision to forgive, but as I've said, our hearts often take time to catch up. The important part here is to avoid anger and bitterness. These emotions eat away at our emotional well-being and can cause anxiety and depression. We often end up the losers. I still have twinges of hurt and anger when I allow myself to think about those who have hurt me over the years. At those moments it is important not to relive or obsess over the offense in our minds. This is a perfect opportunity to think on good things (see Philippians 4:8). I also try to remember those *I* have hurt and ask Jesus to keep my heart soft and open to His work in and through me, which is designed to make me look more like Himself. When I do this, I don't have a lot of time to obsess about the hurt that crops back up now and again.

Forgiving is not cheap or easy but is always required. "If you forgive men when they sin against you, your heavenly Father will also forgive you" (Matthew 6:14). He is most patient with our hearts but does ask us to keep them soft, contrite, and broken. Ultimately He is the wound healer, something no human being will ever be able to do for us.

How Do We Ask for Forgiveness?

What if we're the ones who need forgiveness? Sometimes we hurt someone unintentionally simply because we are unaware of what it means to be sensitive to the heart of another. For instance, offering a friend advice on how she could dress better or improve her hairstyle does little to build her up and encourage her. So often giving advice is more hurtful than helpful—particularly when a person hasn't asked for it.

If a friend's attitude toward you has cooled recently, it might be worth asking yourself whether you've been critical toward her lately. You might also consider whether you've called her, gone to lunch together, or initiated some other activity with her recently. Extroverts, in particular, may feel hurt if their introvert friends don't initiate getting together.

The good news is that God desires to refine us into more tenderhearted women, and He often does this through relationships. Many times I have needed to go to friends and family members to say I am sorry for my tone of voice or hurtful words. I've learned to rely on the Holy Spirit to nudge me when I've been insensitive. I've also learned that it takes time in a relationship to find out how we "come off" to another person, especially when our masks come off and our real selves are revealed.

When we do need to ask for forgiveness, how should we approach the ones we've hurt? In the marriage enrichment seminars that my husband, Gary, and I lead, we suggest that asking for forgiveness should look something like this: "I am sorry for _____ [name the behavior that you recognize and can identify]. I was wrong to _____ [explain how you were wrong and what the offending behavior was]. Please forgive me." This last statement is an invitation, not a demand, and it may take time for those we have wounded to offer true forgiveness. Remember these words and use them when God calls you to do so.

When we ask for forgiveness, we are taking a risk. We don't know how our friend will respond to our request. We have no guarantee that she will love us and forgive us as we desire.

THE REALITY OF RECONCILING

Reconciliation usually requires a repentant heart on the part of the friend who has wounded the other person. A repentant heart is honest, broken, and sees the need for Jesus to help her right the behavior that wounded her friend. Someone with a repentant heart cares deeply that the relationship be restored and will go to great lengths to right the wrong. A repentant heart does not make excuses or blame others for her behavior. Reconciliation then requires the wronged person to extend forgiveness. Reconciliation is an agreement that the friendship will be different—hopefully better—because two people have come out on the other side of forgiveness and hurt. Trust and safety can now be built on the common ground of understanding and love.

When your friend refuses to be honest and take responsibility for her behavior, when her heart becomes hard, and when she does not acknowledge the need to ask you for forgiveness, there will not be reconciliation. Your friendship may be destroyed. Reconciliation also may not be possible if you repent but your friend refuses to accept your apology and forgive you. Either scenario may leave you feeling even more wounded. Please realize that God can take care of this betrayal for you and meet you in the deepest part of your broken heart.

Forgiveness is a process. According to Worthington, it is both a decision and an emotional response.[5] We may make the choice to forgive, but it may be some time before our emotions catch up. Scripture is clear that we are to forgive; however,

God in His grace understands our weaknesses. When I am the weakest and feel I cannot forgive, it is God working through me who accomplishes the forgiveness process. Forgive and be free. Feeling free brings peace and will transform you. Don't miss the miracle.

AND THE FRIENDSHIP GROWS!

Yes, forgiving and being forgiven can lead to growth in a friendship. In fact, the depth of a relationship may depend on the ability to go through forgiveness. God is working out His plans for His good will and for His good purpose. After you and a friend have restored your relationship through forgiveness, ask God what He might have for your friendship now. What is the fresh purpose? Are you any different in how you experience forgiveness in your other relationships? Do you understand your behavior or your personality a little better? Do you understand the heart of your friend more? Is there deeper honesty and trust? These are all the fruit of forgiveness, which can motivate us to work toward forgiveness again when necessary and to pursue friendship like never before.

I have called you friend and you have called me that too
You give me your heart and you entrust your heart to me
You will hurt my heart and I will hurt yours
Who will heal the wounds? Will you? Will I?
Will our Savior intervene when we do not know which
    way to turn?
His promise to us is true
His requirement is simply a broken heart and a truthful
    word
Without these there is no hope
I choose a broken heart, I choose honesty, will you?
We shall reunite, we shall be forgiven and we shall forgive

Let us hope together, let us be honest,
Breaking through the pain
And call each other friend again.
   —CARRIE OLIVER

The grown-up girlfriend . . .

. . . offers grace and compassion when she has been hurt,
knowing that forgiveness and reconciliation can lead to a
stronger relationship.

. . . .

REFLECTION QUESTIONS

1. Are you still carrying a wound from a friendship or another relationship?

2. How do you think being hurt affects you?

3. Have you asked for forgiveness from someone? If not, why do you think you haven't? If you have, what was the process like?

4. Describe what the freedom and peace that come from forgiveness might add to your life.

5. What have you learned in this chapter that you can apply right now in your friendships?

9

☉HE GROWN-UP FRIEND OVERCOMES DESTRUCTIVE FRIENDSHIPS

[Carrie]

What you see and hear depends a good deal
on where you are standing; it also depends
on what kind of person you are.
C. S. LEWIS

I learned that it is the weak who are cruel, and that
gentleness is only expected from the strong.
LEO ROSTEN

Friends come and friends go, but a true friend
sticks by you like family.
PROVERBS 18:24, *THE MESSAGE*

If an enemy were insulting me, I could endure it;
if a foe were raising himself against me,
I could hide from him. But it is you, a man like
myself, my companion, my close friend.
PSALM 55:12-13

Rachel and Claire clicked from the moment they met on
their first day of work at a computer services firm. They were
introduced as they picked up their name tags before the new-
employee orientation meeting. After making small talk about
their shared interest in outdoor sports, they sat down next to

one another. Rachel chose Claire as her partner when the HR director asked her to pick someone to introduce to the rest of the group. Later, during his presentation, they exchanged bemused glances whenever he launched into another long, technical-sounding explanation of some obscure employee benefit. Over bagels later that morning, they discovered that they had graduated a year apart from the same large university and had had several friends in common while on campus.

Before leaving that afternoon, they made plans to meet for lunch later in the week. Soon they began making plans to get together outside of work too. They drank espresso, shopped, and discovered they shared many common interests. They even enrolled in the same master's degree program. When Claire's longtime boyfriend ended their relationship, Rachel was right there to console Claire and try to cheer her up. Everyone thought they had the perfect friendship—and then the trouble began.

In the last chapter, I made the case for granting and seeking forgiveness whenever possible. After all, friendship can bring such goodness and blessing to our hearts. It shouldn't be abandoned without good cause. Yet Erin and I would be remiss if we did not talk candidly about another side of friendship—friendship that becomes destructive.

Being a grown-up friend means recognizing and working on our own unhealthy patterns of relationship, as well as becoming better at picking healthy, godly friends. This is absolutely necessary for building basket one friendships, since this is the level at which the most intimacy and trust are shared. When some of us have experienced a friendship that resulted in pain and confusion, we might have begun to develop an inability to trust. We may even avoid basket one friendships altogether. This chapter is designed to help us develop renewed hope that we can trust again; help us be more aware of the harmful tendencies in ourselves and others; and enable us to choose friends who will love us and be loyal, honest, and committed to working through unhealthy issues and behaviors with us.

THE COMPLEXITIES OF DESTRUCTIVE FRIENDSHIPS

God created something good when He came up with friendship. This truth is the premise of this book! Yet the evil one is still prowling around, seeking to sabotage that which God meant for good. He does that cunningly within the realm of all relationships, including friendships. He desires destruction. When a friendship becomes destructive, often the evil one is involved. He does not want us to enjoy any of the good gifts from God, so he is invested in destroying relationships.

In a destructive friendship, darkness exists at some level, and when darkness exists, the heart closes. That makes it almost impossible to grow to look like and become like Christ. Because Satan is the great liar, we may not even be aware our hearts are closed. For a long time, I could not see the pride that was keeping me from making new friends in Siloam Springs.

By the time a friendship becomes destructive, some intimacy has already been established and a bond formed. Often in the beginning of a friendship, we just don't see the warning signs. That's because when two people pursue a friendship, they often put on their best behavior, just as in dating! They may enjoy lots of laughter, positive feelings, and little conflict, and they usually spend hours talking and doing things together. They may even discover a shared spirituality. This results in trust, empathy, vulnerability, communication, and common interests that create a strong bond. It is only when a bond is formed that some relationships begin to take on a pervasive,

nagging negativity. Something does not feel quite right, and
conflict becomes more prevalent. One or both friends may feel
drained, misunderstood, and off balance. In most cases, however, the friends still have good times together. But remember:
Good times do not equal, nor are they the same as, the healthy
intimacy God intends for us to experience. Good times alone
are not the basis for a grown-up friendship.

It's wise to build close friendships slowly, which gives us
time to set up appropriate boundaries around our hearts.
Boundaries are helpful in preventing us from becoming
involved in destructive relationships. Sharing our hearts too
quickly and succumbing to pressure from a new friend are
warning signs that a friendship may become too needy or
destructive.

IDENTIFYING THE NEGATIVE ASPECTS OF A DESTRUCTIVE FRIENDSHIP

The word *destructive* can be defined this way: "To ruin
thoroughly, to spoil; to tear down or break up."[1] Destructive
relationships are destructive in part because something that
has been built is being torn down. Many of us know there
are certain types of people we would never choose to form a
bond with, but the friend with whom we have a falling-out in
a destructive friendship rarely fits that description. We enjoy
our friend's company, which is why a bond formed in the first
place.

Rachel and Claire enjoyed each other from day one. Their
differences seemed few; they quickly came to expect laughter
and long conversations whenever they were together. They had
walked through difficulties and crises. So what was the problem? With time, pervasive insecurities crept into the relationship.

One of the first signs of a destructive relationship is a friend's
need to make your friendship exclusive. She may insist that you

not spend time with anyone else or demand a lot of your time. She may need to be *the* best friend. She likely will resist your attempts to resolve conflict in a healthy way. We'll identify a number of other red flags as we move through this chapter.

Destructive friendships generally involve a dance of the manipulator and the manipulated. In her book *Emotional Blackmail*, Susan Forward identifies six deadly symptoms that warn us that something may be very wrong with a friendship.[2] Here is an adapted explanation of the pattern that ultimately leads to a destructive cycle in a friendship and breaks down the bond between two people.

A DESTRUCTIVE CYCLE

The cycle often begins when a friend displays a **demanding spirit**. After going through a crisis that deeply hurt her, Claire began expecting Rachel to spend much of her weekend with her, whether shopping, going to the movies, or just hanging out with friends at one of their apartments. She made Rachel feel that if she could not live up to her demands, she was not a "real friend." Rachel felt very guilty whenever Claire communicated in this manner.

The message may be direct or it may be subtle—perhaps even soft—but it is always the same: "You need to do this for me." Rachel heard the message that she needed to be more loving and more available. If she didn't talk more and listen to Claire's needs, there would be negative consequences.

Again, a relationship becomes destructive when such demands are made subtly and selfishly. So how do we distinguish between a healthy friendship, in which a friend brings up a legitimate issue, and a destructive friendship, in which unreasonable demands are being made? If you're wrestling with this, ask yourself whether you feel guilty, ashamed, and as if you just can't live up to your friend's expectations, no matter what you do. In a destructive friendship, conflict will not be resolved, no matter how hard you try.

As a result, the demands of a friend in a destructive relationship often elicit **resistance**. In this case, Rachel allowed herself to feel uncomfortable with Claire's demands. Since she wasn't sure how to respond, she began avoiding Claire, getting angry, and trying to distance herself. Because good boundaries were never set and Rachel and Claire never learned how to resolve conflict, their friendship turned into an unhealthy dance.

After sensing Rachel's resistance, Claire put on the **pressure**. She tried to manipulate Rachel even further. She accused Rachel of being uncommitted to their friendship and no longer acting as a best friend should. Claire tried to pressure Rachel into spending more time with her to show her that she really cared. Feeling guilty, Rachel complied. She didn't trust her ability to discern and make wise choices. *After all,* she thought to herself, *Claire is my "best friend," and best friends go the extra mile, don't they?* Such questions begin to haunt the person being manipulated.

The destructive cycle turns **threatening**. When Rachel called Claire one day to say she would have to cancel their plans to meet for dinner because her grandmother had been admitted to the hospital, Claire reacted angrily and threatened to find another best friend who "really wants intimacy." Throughout the next week, Rachel called to check in with Claire a few times. Each time, Claire threw in little digs about how she suspected Rachel was incapable of intimacy and could not possibly understand how badly Claire had been hurt by those closest to her. Rachel now felt as if an ultimatum had been presented to her: Either meet Claire's demands or expect to lose her friendship.

At this point Rachel **complied**. Remembering the good times they'd shared—she'd never had a friend to whom she felt closer and entrusted more secrets—Rachel gave in and tried to find out how she could meet Claire's needs in ways that would get her to stop pressuring and threatening her. Like most people caught in destructive friendship patterns, Rachel and Claire shared a basket one friendship, and both had a real fear of losing the relationship. In Rachel's case, this motivated her unhealthy compliance to Claire's demands.

Rather than resolving the conflict, however, Rachel and Claire simply **repeated** it. Because they'd never learned godly conflict resolution, the unhealthy cycle had not been eliminated by Rachel's capitulation. Before long, she had disappointed Claire and the cycle began again.

Fear on both sides is at the core of destructive friendships: fear of change, fear of loss, fear of rejection, and fear of losing power. And what drives the manipulator? Often she has a history of anxiety and inadequacy. Look at this truth from Scripture: "There is no fear in love; but perfect love casts out fear, because fear involves torment. But he who fears has not been made perfect in love" (1 John 4:18, NKJV). Perfect love, grown-up love, does not produce fear.

When you're caught in a destructive cycle, the most difficult task is identifying what part each of you is playing and then deciding what you need to do differently. Much of this corresponds to the grown-up skills we've already discussed in this book, such as setting good boundaries (chapter 5), communicating effectively (chapter 7), and resolving conflicts productively (chapters 7 and 8).

Breaking the cycle always requires at least one friend to identify her part and begin to do something differently. For instance, if I see that I manipulate to get my way, I can begin to change. I may even confess to my friend that I have been trying to manipulate her to do what I want out of my own insecurity and fear. If I am the manipulated one, I must give up my fear that I will lose the relationship if I don't comply. Remember, there is no fear in love. Setting loving boundaries and seeking to resolve conflict in a healthy, loving way should not compromise the friendship. A destructive cycle can be broken.

Of course, the manipulator may not respond to our overtures in a healthy way. When we don't give in to fear, however, we don't panic over the possibility of losing the relationship and we recognize that we are not in control of another person's choices.

On the other hand, what if we decide to ignore the problem and hope it goes away on its own? If boundaries, good communication, and conflict resolution are not instituted, the cycle will begin again. This is growth inhibiting, it is sad and wearing, and it does not bring glory to God—the bottom-line purpose of any relationship. It may be time to let this relationship go.

Negative Behaviors That Prevent Intimacy

Not only may we fall into destructive cycles, we are all capable of exhibiting negative behaviors that keep our friendships from growing and being all that God designed them to be. These behaviors may be triggered by past negative interactions with our families of origin or others, our identity development or lack of it, components of our personalities, and sexual or physical abuse.

In her book *When Friendship Hurts*, Jan Yager identifies twenty-one types of negative friends, including these five common ones:[3]

The Rival: As their friendship developed, Jane realized that her friend Susan wanted to have whatever she had. Jane had a happy marriage, and Susan was clearly jealous of that. Susan also went to great lengths to get what Jane had. After Jane announced that she would be running for the presidency of a local service club, she was stunned when Susan told her she would be running against her. The rival competes for what her friend has—her clothes, her children, her job, and quite often other friends.

The Blood-Sucker: Chris needed Becky for everything! Becky often felt she could not begin to meet all Chris's needs. Chris wanted more time for conversation, and she expected Becky to heal her hurts, past and present. Chris did not like Becky to spend time with others and frequently would sabotage Becky's time with other friends by inviting herself to be a part of Becky's outings with them. Chris had an unhealthy dependence on Becky.

The Copycat: In the grown-up friendship, each person has her own identity. While we often choose friends with similarities to us, we do not honor God when we try to become another person. We can wear some of the same things, have similar thoughts, and have similar lifestyles, but in the destructive relationship, a friend will not tolerate any differences. You might see this happening if your friend starts wearing what you wear most of the time, goes to all the places you go, and wants to be friends with all your other friends.

Sally often felt in trouble if she resisted her friend Barb's attempts to imitate her. Barb bought clothes similar to Sally's. She'd try to have coffee with someone after Sally told her that she had just met that person at their favorite coffee shop. Others noticed Barb's behavior and made negative comments such as, "It seems those two cannot make up their own minds or exist apart from one another."

Not surprisingly, when Sally kindly told Barb she did not like having so many of the same things, Barb tried to shame her by saying that if she were a better friend she would want them to be alike.

The Controller: Control can be as simple as needing to have our own way all the time. We are acting as controllers if we make all the decisions in relationships—where to go and what to do. People with strong opinions and leadership tendencies easily fall into this role. When a controller connects with an overly dependent person, both their identities are compromised. Not only is the one being controlled pressured to change, but the controller's identity is wrapped up in her desire to call all the shots. Only when she gives up this tendency will she look more like what Christ intended her to be.

Other types of control are more subtle. If we fear losing a relationship, we may try to manage that fear by controlling the relationship. Both friends can easily fall into this trap. Remember Rachel and Claire? Once the destructive cycle began, both tried to control the other. Claire tried to coerce Rachel into meeting her unhealthy needs; Rachel reacted by distancing herself and avoiding Claire as a way to control and get away from Claire's demands. All controlling behaviors are destructive and must be addressed before a friendship can grow.

The Caretaker: The destructive and negative caretaker takes care of her friend in order to meet her own needs—not those of her friend. In other words, her caretaking role is part of her identity rather than true service.

When Lynn was ill, Mindy insisted that she be the only one to take her friend's kids to school. When Lynn wanted her friends' input into how she could redecorate her kitchen, Mindy insisted on being the one to go to Home Depot with her. While her help was not all bad, she prevented Lynn from allowing other friends to offer their input and help.

The caretaker often believes she can do caretaking better than other people. She sends the message to other friends that she knows us best and that she will take care of our needs. She intends to be sure no one else gets close to us. However, the caretaker does not show true mercy. Mercy is a gift with no strings attached, but the caretaker will be hurt or angry if a friend rejects her advances. Remember, the caretaker is really invested in getting her own caretaking needs met through others.

While painful, it is crucial that we be able to pinpoint these behaviors in ourselves and our friends. Gaining this insight and wisdom will help our relationships rather than hinder them. For several years now, I have been asking the Lord to humble me. I know I can be a controller. I like to go certain places, drive certain ways, and organize in my way, and at times I have thought everyone was entitled to my opinion!

I've learned, however, that when I sincerely ask to be humbled, God will do it. While it's sometimes painful, I am thankful for His work in my life. I enjoy myself more when I am more gentle, soft, and less concerned about whether something is done my way. It is freeing and peaceful. My relationships have taken on a new flavor. Yes, I still revert to needing control at times, but I usually identify this trap right away and call it for what it is. I am sure my friends and my husband appreciate the intentionality with which I've been working to eliminate this destructive behavior.

At the core of our sinful natures, we all are capable of one or all of these negative behaviors. When we are able to identify them in ourselves or our friends, one of two things will happen. Either we will make the difficult changes that lead to a healthier friendship or we will choose to sweep the offending behavior under the rug. Because we cannot resolve the issues without addressing the underlying anxiety, fear, and hurt, we sometimes try to maintain the laughter and fun at all costs. That means avoiding difficult change and forfeiting the opportunity to change the relationship in any meaningful and long-lasting way.

But the price is high. We will still have that nagging sense that something is wrong in the relationship and that the destructive patterns are not being resolved. Intimacy is compromised, and we cannot break out of the adolescent stage of friendship. We have not grown up.

WHEN TRUST HAS BEEN BROKEN

The ultimate mark of a destructive friendship is the experience of betrayal. There is little that compares to the deep hurt of betrayal. You may find yourself wincing at that word even now. Your heart wells up with painful sensations because you know betrayal firsthand.

We can only be betrayed if we have trusted a friend at a deep level. If we have not risked trust or allowed ourselves a basket one friendship, we may not have experienced betrayal. A common form of betrayal is when a friend tells another friend something we've told her in confidence. Sometimes it is even worse.

Claire eventually tired of Rachel and wanted to move on to a new relationship. Though their friendship hadn't been healthy, it had lasted a long time, more than ten years. Rachel was devastated when she saw that Claire was starting a relationship much like theirs with someone new.

An end to a relationship is not necessarily betrayal, but Claire said hurtful and untrue things about Rachel and her family to her new friend. Rachel grieved and felt hurt because she had tried so hard to live up to Claire's expectations. Yet eventually she realized that the pain had some benefits: She saw that she had failed to please the Lord in many ways in this relationship, so the end of their friendship was an opportunity to grow and change. She began looking for friends whom she could really trust.

So what does trust look like? To trust means we believe in the honesty and the integrity of our friend. When we trust, we risk putting our hearts into the hands of another person to be held gently, softly, and tenderly. We believe that our hearts are safe with them and that they will not betray us.

Betrayal looks like this: Our hearts discover that most of what we thought was true is not, and we feel as if our hearts have been crushed in the hands of our friend. We find out that we have been misled and deceived, perhaps from the beginning of the relationship. Betrayal is wrapped in darkness and requires a great deal of effort before its destruction can be repaired. In fact, such a friendship can be restored only through honesty, brokenness, repentance, forgiveness, and a commitment to change. Good communication and conflict resolution skills are essential.

When betrayal is not worked through, the relationship often ends, as we will discuss in more detail in the next chapter. Betrayal can produce great feelings of loss and grief. Often the betrayed friend is left with a sense that it will never be safe to trust again. (She may even question God and ask how He could possibly have allowed this hurtful experience.) Betrayal surprises us every time. We do not see it coming. We would not have predicted it. Betrayal is probably one of the evil one's greatest weapons to destroy relationships.

I confess I did not understand this type of deep hurt until it happened to me. I now know what it's like to become angry, grief stricken, defeated, and gun shy about trusting another friend again as a result of betrayal. Yet in many ways I am thankful for what God taught me through this experience. You see, no person can give us everything we want. Jesus is the only one who can fill us with life, so our hearts must first crave to be filled up with His love. Only then can we go through hurtful times and come out on the other side, able to forgive and, yes, even trust again. Henri Nouwen explained what that meant to him: "The interruption of friendship forced me to enter the basement of my soul and look directly at what was hidden there, to choose, in the face of it all, not death but life."[4]

GROWTH AFTER A DESTRUCTIVE RELATIONSHIP

A part of living the Christian life is growing up in Christ. When we walk closely and intimately with Jesus, we grow to look more and more like Him in the way we love—with tenderness, mercy, kindness, and gentleness. We also become increasingly wise and discerning. As painful as it is, a destructive friendship can mold us into greater Christlikeness.

We learn that, though we are called to love all people, we are not called to be intimate with everyone. We become wiser about choosing whom we will trust to the point of deep intimacy. So how should we proceed after being betrayed?

Let Christ fill your heart first. When we believe that only Christ can love us completely (see Ephesians 3:17-19), we are able to love others in a more godly and healthy way. We are also much more lovable people!

It may also help to consider Christ's example: Our Lord experienced betrayal at deep levels. Knowing this and embracing His wounds can help us with our own woundedness.

Become wise and discerning. Every relationship is an opportunity for growth and learning. We can embrace these opportunities, even the painful ones, and learn from them. As we learn, we are better at discerning God's purpose for each relationship and deciding which ones have the potential to be healthy and bring Him glory.

Be willing to trust even after betrayal. When we decide never to trust again after being betrayed, we are actually trying to gain control. Yet control is only an illusion. While on this earth, we have little control, dear ones! What we do have a choice over is whether or not we will walk with God. We have a similar choice when it comes to trust. Deciding never to trust again is usually our effort to protect ourselves from pain and hurt. Yet if a hurtful friendship doesn't get us, something else will. (Sorry to be so blunt, but we do live in a fallen world!)

I, too, am tempted to trust guardedly. But I know that ultimately I will be the one who loses if I make that choice. I will lose out on the goodness of friendship. I might even be a better, more sensitive friend after walking the road of betrayal and learning to trust again.

Seek out nondestructive friends. How can you know when you've found her? The nondestructive friend brings her own identity to the relationship; she supports, rather than caretakes; she is honest and truthful but not critical; she can make decisions for herself but does not need to make decisions for everyone around her. She honors your other friendships while having a clear vision of the purpose God had when He brought the two of you together. She does not try to manipulate you but rather desires to encourage you. She believes the best about you. She forgives but does not accept nonrepentant, recurring destructive behavior. You can trust your heart to her. She will hold it well.

The grown-up girlfriend . . .

. . . addresses her own unhealthy patterns of relating and becomes wiser about picking healthy, godly friends.

· ·

REFLECTION QUESTIONS

1. What destructive behaviors have you identified within yourself that you might bring into relationships?

2. If you are currently in a destructive friendship, what can you do right now to bring about change? What information on boundaries and communication from the previous chapters might be helpful?

3. What do you think God is trying to teach you as you identify destructive behaviors in yourself or in your friend?

4. Have you ever been deeply betrayed? If so, how is that affecting your current friendships?

THE GROWN-UP FRIEND KNOWS
WHEN TO LET GO

[Carrie]

If your friendship is only for a season,
then let it be a full season.
WILLIAM AND PATRICIA COLEMAN[1]

He who covers over an offense promotes love, but
whoever repeats the matter separates close friends.
PROVERBS 17:9

I am not the type who buys something to make a memory. Not long ago, though, I made an exception. I'd been visiting Santa Fe, New Mexico, in the autumn with some dear friends. While in a shop with them, I bought a pair of long, dangly silver earrings. I liked how they looked, but I particularly liked them because they were a reminder of the memorable time we had had together that week. We enjoyed coffee and music in the morning and then spent time shopping and hiking trails ablaze with the turning aspen leaves later each day. I'll never forget the incredible view of colorful trees and rugged peaks that we witnessed after hiking to the top of a mountain.

Several weeks ago, I discovered that one of the earrings was missing. (This often happens when I have been shopping and pulling clothes on and off over my head. I guess one solution would be to shop less!) I was depressed by my discovery. While I remain close to those friends and the memory of our trip remains clear, the symbol of our adventure is gone and cannot be replaced.

Of course, losing an earring—even one so closely associated with a precious memory—is nothing compared to losing a friendship. When we are children, broken friendships aren't really that uncommon. Little girls often call someone their best friend one week, only to move on to a new best friend the following week! Some of us remember that pain all too well.

We might agree that the broken friendships we experience in adulthood are at least as painful. Over the years in my counseling office, a number of women have told me their stories of broken friendship. Being a tender sort, I always feel compassion and often help by providing insights into dealing with these situations in healthy ways. It has become a whole new world for me since I, too, experienced a broken friendship, an experience that has wounded my heart to the very core.

I was devastated as I felt my friend slipping away from me and my heart. I did not always handle the situation well. In hindsight I realize I could have allowed Jesus to have been much more a part of our relationship.

Perhaps you have lost a friendship through conflict or betrayal or because of a root of bitterness that began to grow and was never resolved. Sometimes we must accept that we cannot control another person or our life circumstances and may need to let go of a relationship, at least for now.

"When people walk away from you: let them walk," suggests author and pastor T. D. Jakes. "People leave you because they are not joined to you. And if they are not joined to you, you can't make them stay. Let them go. And it doesn't mean that they are a bad person; it just means that their part in the story is over. And you've got to know when people's part in your story is over so that you don't keep trying to raise the dead."

Even when, with God's help, we release our friend, losing a basket one friendship is a great and deep loss that takes time to work through. In this chapter we'll look more closely at the loss of an intimate friendship. While we'll begin by considering the friendship that collapses because of betrayal, we will look at other factors that can end a basket one friendship. Sometimes we simply grow apart emotionally; at other times, we are physically separated by a move or even illness and death. As difficult as this topic is, particularly if it brings back the hurt of a lost friendship, we encourage you to keep reading. You can trust Jesus to provide good for you in future relationships or even in the present ones. Sometimes we become so stuck in our losses that we cannot see the good people He has brought into our lives to love and befriend us. Through the psalmist, the Lord reminds us that He fills our lives with good things (see Psalm 103:5).

TYPES OF FRIENDSHIP LOSSES

Broken Intimacy/Betrayal

Unless we take deliberate steps to repair a destructive relationship, it almost always ends up broken. Often the destructive relationship involves betrayal, and betrayal is not easily mended. Is restoration possible? Oh yes, but only with a great measure of forgiveness, change, and a broken and contrite heart. The truth is, this rarely happens, and when it doesn't, we may feel as if our hearts have been stomped on. We grieve as we let go of something we thought was safe, secure, and forever.

When we've been betrayed, we need to turn to Jesus, or we

can end up bitter and angry. We can put walls up to prevent anyone else from getting too close to us. After all, she might hurt us too. We can even become angry at God. So often we ask, "How could you let this happen, God?" In His mercy and grace, God lets us ask Him that question. But if we keep asking it, we stay stuck! I strongly believe that the "Why, God?" question is ultimately Satan's way of keeping us depressed, discouraged, angry, bitter, and separated from the intimacy Christ wants to offer us. Some better questions to ask are these: *How could I have done this relationship better? What can I learn from this painful experience and apply to my other relationships?* Only in humility will we hear God's answers. Loss, grief, and betrayal will chip away at our flesh and make us look more like Him. In that process, painful as it can be, there is hope for even deeper and greater relationships.

Growing Apart

While betrayal often results in the dramatic loss of a friendship, sometimes friends simply allow themselves to grow apart. All relationships require time and effort and nurture. If we've neglected a friendship for a while, it can generally be repaired—assuming both parties are willing. On the other hand, if we don't deliberately devote some of our energy to a basket one friendship, we'll almost certainly lose some of the intimacy.

Sometimes we grow apart when we allow other relationships to replace the ones we have. We grow apart if we once shared Jesus deeply but become less enthusiastic about this spiritual facet of the relationship. We grow apart when we lose sight of our shared vision and purpose for the relationship.

Some women say they grow apart because their friend is now in a different season of life. I have a hard time accepting this. I think we can be friends with women who are not living their lives exactly as we are. I think we are the richer for it. If we go through life seeking out only those who are in the same place we are—whether we're a mother who stays home with our small children or a single working woman—then we limit what God can do to stretch us and show us body life through relationships with other women. I love asking questions, dreaming, processing, and talking about ideas with others. In fact, I can do all those things with anybody! I believe this is possible because I've allowed myself to seek friendships with women from all walks of life—older, younger, married, single, with or without children.

I've already mentioned how I came to accept one of my friend's more introverted nature. I should also tell you that she is not a coffee drinker, while I enjoy few things more than sitting down for a talk with a friend at a coffeehouse. Cheryl does not like coffee, but she has learned to drink chai tea just so we can connect at my favorite coffee place!

Still, growing apart happens. When it does, take the opportunity to assess what is going on. Who grew away from whom? You and your friend will need to communicate and decide whether you will work together to restore your friendship to a deep level. You might choose to make a "basket shift" or even end the relationship. Growing apart can be less painful when two people agree that their relationship has taken a shift. Still, growing apart represents a loss. We no longer can count on that person being there for us in the same way.

A Move

Moving away from the known, the comfortable, and the safe can be unsettling at the least and grief producing at the worst. I remember moving away from my family's farm to college. None of my friends from my small town ventured to the university with me. Suddenly I was in a dorm room with Miss Nebraska, who came from Omaha (the big city in Nebraska). Soon I joined a sorority full of more young women and attended classes with at least one hundred students in each one. For quite a while I felt alone and lost, and wanted desperately to cling to something I knew.

Since that move, I have married and our family has moved six times in twenty-five years. Before moving to our current home in Arkansas, we lived for twelve years in Denver. Though I'm confident God led us to Siloam Springs, years later I still cry sometimes because I'm missing my precious Denver friends. We e-mail, we write, we call, and we visit, but nothing replaces the tangibility of being able to spontaneously stop over to sit at the kitchen counter of a dear friend or grab lunch or coffee together. This is a loss. People cannot replace other people. We were created to bond and experience closeness, but as we venture out, we risk loss. In fact, I have known women who keep themselves from getting too close to others because they know they will move again. I wonder if that is really what God wants for us. I don't think so. Each time we risk loving, we are the richer for it, even though it hurts to say good-bye. When we do move, just a little bit more of our hearts have to rely on Jesus to fill them and to heal us and guide us through the loss as we trust that we will find new friendships.

Illness and Death

The relationship that ends because of death is rarely talked about and yet needs tender, thoughtful processing. What can we possibly gain by losing a friend through death? I do not know what the future holds for me. I am walking a journey right now that could end in loss for my friends. Yet I am constantly amazed by my friends' outpouring of love and hope.

My friends Jane and Cheryl have been willing to share their hearts regarding their journeys with me, as well as their own journeys with the death of someone close to them. Jane tells her story first:

> *My mother was my best friend. I remember how difficult it was when we moved to Iowa, so far away from her Ohio home. Then came the dreadful and unexpected news of the astrocytoma in her brain in October 1991. During the early stages of her cancer, I remember just praying for healing—a miracle in her case. By early winter, it became apparent that God's path for healing for her would be an eternal one. She was brave and flew out by herself to visit us in the spring. I remember her crawling up the stairs on her hands and knees because she wasn't stable enough to walk up them.*
>
> *The next time I saw her it was summer, and she was unable to walk at all. I would visit every few weeks, and we just tried to treasure the time that we had. We shared together from a little book called* God Is Enough *by Hannah Whitall Smith. The phrase that I clung to during this time was from Psalm 62:8: "Trust in him at all times." I continually felt God saying to me, Jane, do you trust Me in this? Do you really trust Me? And I resounded from my heart—yes. It was during this difficult stage that my faith grew immensely, that I learned that I am not in control and that our lives are in God's hands.*
>
> *The next few months were a blur as we moved from Iowa to Indiana—a blessing to be closer to my mother but still stressful. We moved into our first home, but my*

mom never got a chance to see it. Her health rapidly declined over the next few months—each time I saw her she was faded a bit more. I was with my mom when she took her last breath, and I can honestly say it was the most peaceful experience of my life. I felt the presence of God in that room and knew He had taken her home. I miss my mom immensely, and my life is not the same without her. But I have hope that I will see her again and will spend eternity with her.

As I reflect on cancer reentering my life through you, my dear friend Carrie, I have heard God again say to me, Do you trust Me? I have prayed vigorously for God to heal you, and I use my imagination to see those cells dying one by one and my dear Carrie restored. I spend time waiting quietly before God for my hope is in Him [see Lamentations 3:25], and I want to share that hope with you and support you in any way that I can. Your fight has brought up some memories that are at times painful but are also hopeful—no matter what, God is enough and He is in control!

Cheryl writes about the loss of her friend and brother, Kim, who died of cancer:

I believe it's a gift to begin the grieving process for a loved one before they end their lives here on earth. To lose a family member or friend through death is life altering.

I know cancer is what ultimately brought my brother, Kim, to a recognition of his need for the Savior. Our relationship was transformed through Kim's cancer too. We both felt the urgency to establish a deeper, truer relationship. When we spent time together we were able to talk openly about our love for one another, our hopes for our families, and our fears about the future. Our relationship was qualitatively richer. Cancer gave us the opportunity (by the faith it birthed in Kim and the faith it stretched in me) to talk out loud about what is most real and true in this world.

With you, Carrie, this journey has been different. Kim's faith was brand new. Your faith has been cured by the weather: the wind, the rain, the storms, and certainly by the sunshine God has brought into your life through years of actively pursuing God. I believe God has been preparing you for this time. He has been working hard in your life to keep your face turned upward, and I believe He has been richly pleased by your faithfulness.

I realize that our time together here on earth might be shorter. There is the aspect of my faith being stretched and cured by this tempest called "pancreatic cancer." Will God heal you? He can and He will as He chooses to!

You know, when I was little I had warts all over my hand. A lady from my church told me that when she was a little girl she had warts too. She said an adult "bought her warts away" from her. From that point on she believed that her warts would all go away. And they did. So that lady did the same thing for me. She gave me a nickel and "bought my warts away." I believed her. All my warts went away—every single one of them. And I still have the nickel!

Carrie, I'm not superstitious, and I know God can't be bought. But I also know faith in God changes everything. So in a very real way, I believe the same thing for your cancer as I did for my little-girl warts. Nothing is impossible with God!

For believers, the hopeful news about facing illness and possibly even death with a friend is the tangible peace we can hold on to regardless of the outcome. We can look forward to eternity, when we will again hold the precious people whom we've lost. When we're reunited, we'll feel as if we've been separated for only the blink of an eye. Colossians 1:5 talks of "the hope that is stored up for you in heaven," and one of the joys we can anticipate is being with our loved ones again. For me this truth does not take the incredible sting out of death, but it allows me to invite God to meet me with His healing hand and merciful heart. And it opens me up to drink in the love and prayer offered by my friends.

Dealing with Loss

Whether or not we lose a friend to death, the grief we feel over the loss of an intimate friendship can be intense. Think about it. This person was a constant presence in our lives. We may have talked on the phone and sipped coffee, shopped, worked, and perhaps even taken care of one another's kids. We also walked through many of life's major changes together—whether at work, with our kids, or at social events. The friendship may end quickly or die a slow death, but the resulting void leaves grief and sorrow. After such a great loss, many of us lose hope that we will ever have a soul mate friend, a basket number one friend, again. We know that people are not replaceable.

It is important to allow ourselves to feel the grief, the loss, and the confusion and to cry out to God frequently concerning the pain we feel. He loves when we come to Him seeking His love, His shelter, His grace, and His strength. Walking through any type of grief is an opportunity to grow, to change, and to become more Christlike. Though we may still feel abandoned, eventually we may get to a point where we're okay with this loneliness because we've come to understand that Jesus is the ultimate lover of our hearts and that only He can fill us with what we really need.

Dealing with loss is almost always more tolerable when we have other healthy relationships in our lives. If we have not developed other friendships, we may feel very alone. If we are married, this may be an opportunity to grow closer to our husband. Often women turn to other women for love and support at the expense of their marriage relationship. We don't believe that is what God had in mind. Our marriage relationship should come first. It can fill us, support us, and nurture us in ways that friendships with women cannot. We can take our grief and sorrow to our husbands and let them know what we need from them. We might ask them to listen as we talk, to hold us, or to let us cry with them. We need to let them know, though, that we realize they cannot "fix" grief and we don't expect them to. We can then ask them to pray for us as we walk through this valley of pain.

I grew very close to Gary as I walked through the pain of losing a friend. While Gary and I considered each other best friends before, this grief brought us even closer. Gary was tender with me on the hard days, and he also encouraged me to get out and befriend others. He was my cheerleader and gave me great wisdom when I needed it. God wants to use the marriage relationship for healing and for bonding.

Whether or not you're married, do things with people. Do not gossip about the broken friendship, but get out and do some things you enjoy. Let go of the expectation that new friendships will feel like the friendship that has been broken— they won't, at least not right away. Just as you probably spent years nurturing the friendship you've lost, you'll need to spend time cultivating and caring for new friendships. It takes time to build trust and safety in a relationship.

I know it can be physically and emotionally draining to reach out to others, yet I've also found it can be worth it—especially if we believe that God is at work when we do so.

ON THE OTHER SIDE OF LOSS

Let's face it—it is much more fun to talk about the positives of friendship. Processing the end of a friendship is painful. It can leave us feeling hopeless rather than hopeful. It's easy to become insecure and listen to the evil one, who tries to convince us that we will never again experience close friendship and that it is not worth trusting or investing our hearts in someone else. I know that firsthand: Following a move, I've always found it hard to reach out to new people because I so long for my old friends.

We can embrace a different perspective, however, when we recognize that even the loss of friendship is an opportunity to grow. We can grow in our intimacy with Christ as we learn to trust Him more deeply. Hope says that God has something good for us in the future. God will use even this painful experience to overcome our weak areas.

As I mentioned in the last chapter, I've had to wrestle with my need for control for years! God finally has gotten my attention, and I am now waving the white flag. I surrender! Losing a close friend and getting cancer just about convinced me of my lack of control. While change is not comfortable and often hurts, I have relished the peace that giving up control brings. I have much less anxiety. Whether we are too controlling or too dependent (or we face some other issue altogether), we inhibit what God wants to do in us and through us until we allow Him to change us. Sometimes that comes only through pain.

Letting go of a relationship may bring tears for a season, but dear ones, know that God will not leave our hearts empty.

When we let go, something else is always out there just waiting to be embraced.

The grown-up girlfriend . . .

. . . expects God to use the loss of a friendship to refine her weaknesses and draw her closer to Him.

. . . .

REFLECTION QUESTIONS

1. Have you ever lost a friendship? If so, what was the cause? Explain how you responded and what the process of grieving that friendship looked like. What did you learn from that experience?

2. Have you ever left a friendship, causing pain to someone else? If so, what did you learn from it?

3. How do you typically walk through grief in your life? Think about other losses you have experienced in order to answer this question.

4. Have you ever repaired a friendship after a period of loss? How did that happen?

5. What would you say is the most important thing you learned from this chapter?

.

The Grown-Up Friend Reaches Out in Crisis

[Carrie]

Two are better than one because they have a good
return for their labor. For if either of them falls, the
one will lift up his companion. But woe to the one
who falls when there is not another to lift him up.
ECCLESIASTES 4:9-10, NASB

The greatest love is shown when a person lays
down his life for his friends.
JOHN 15:13, TLB

Perhaps, like me, you grew up in a family in which it seemed
crisis did not happen. Every day was pretty much the same
in our home. My sisters and I got up, had breakfast, went
to school, did our after-school activities, and came home to
a quiet evening of dinner and studying or watching TV. We
could always count on our parents' being there. Neither they
nor any of our friends' parents divorced. The closest we ever
came to disaster while growing up was the day we learned that
a nearby family had lost a teen to cancer. One of our grand-
fathers also died of cancer fairly young, but I wasn't close to
him and do not remember much about his illness and death.
All in all, my life seemed trial free.

True crisis and tragedy became real to me later in life. (Some would say having three sons was my first crisis. At times I would have agreed—but that is a different book and different story!) My first true crisis began when my husband, Gary, was diagnosed with oral cancer at age thirty-eight. Since then he has had five episodes, including one stage 3 occurrence. My mother and sister both have battled breast cancer as well.

Then, in May 2005, the crisis was mine. I had been sick since November of 2004, but the physicians could not identify the problem right away. In my heart, I believe God allowed this journey to unfold just as it did. In the days before the diagnosis I went from 122 pounds (I had already lost weight) to 113; at my lowest I struggled to keep above 100 pounds. That is when the doctor did more blood work and ordered another CT scan. Not long after, I received the dreaded call: "Mrs. Oliver, could you meet with the doctor today at noon to talk about your CT scan?"

As Gary and I sat in the doctor's office, I felt as if I were having an out-of-body experience. As I looked at the image of the tumor and tried to listen to what the doctor was saying, I sank further and further into the arms of my husband.

Pancreatic cancer has a 4 percent survival rate. I did not know this in the beginning because I refused to look at any Web sites on this stinky cancer. I refused to be a statistic, but I saw the concern in people's eyes and knew I had a long, tough battle to fight.

Several weeks ago I heard a message at church on how we learn endurance while going through trials. The apostle James began his letter by reminding us that when our endurance is tested we have a chance to grow so that we can be strong in character. "Consider it pure joy," he said, "whenever you face trials of many kinds, because you know that the testing of your faith develops perseverance. Perseverance must finish its work so that you may be mature and complete, not lacking anything" (James 1:2-4).

There it is again, the idea of growing and maturing. Grown-up girlfriends have the opportunity to grow with someone in her trial and to bring joy in the midst of grief, pain, doubt, and anger. Often a suffering person is not thinking about growing or enduring. Instead she is thinking, *Why, God?* or *How will I make it through?* or *Is anybody really there for me?* As James points out, crisis can be an opportunity to learn new and better ways of coping. However, it can also be lethal if we stay in despair and fall into depression, alienation, and hopelessness. Sometimes having a grown-up girlfriend to walk with through the crisis can make all the difference.

RESPONDING TO CRISIS

Before we can actually be supportive and loving friends, however, we need to understand what a crisis is and how widely its ripple effects can be felt. Crisis is defined by Webster's dictionary as, "a crucial time or turning point." Crisis is anything that throws us off balance—perhaps even into a state of panic or defeat. Crisis can produce trauma; it can be a deeply wounding event that leads to feelings of sadness, emptiness, depression, anxiety, or anger. Often, those in crisis feel as if they've lost the ability to cope.

The loneliness in the midst of crisis feels almost unbearable at times, as if we are the only ones who could possibly be feeling as we are. That is a test right there. Can we believe that someone loves us enough to come alongside and walk the trial with us? Can we ask for help when we need it and go to God when only He can meet our deepest needs?

Immediately after receiving the diagnosis, I knew I needed Jesus and people right away. That's not true of everyone in crisis; in particular, introverts may feel differently about their friends' involvement. I have friends who have gone into a time of isolation when crises hit. Before reaching out, they need time to look inside themselves to figure out what their next step should be. Ultimately people in crisis long to connect.

Sometimes when we're in crisis, we really grasp the truth of what God has to say in His Word about joy in the midst of trials. At other times, we're angry at God for allowing our hardships. We feel as if our lives have been "thrown off," so we do not feel in control. We may work hard at trying to get some control back. Often our perspective becomes distorted. We lose sight of reality or we are groping for what reality is. One of the things many of us have in common is that we long for the moments before the crisis hit: the moment before the diagnosis; before our spouse asked for the divorce or told us that he was having an affair; before we found out our child is alcohol and drug dependent and had been lying to us for years; before we heard of the car crash that killed a family member or close friend. We so want to go back, but we can't.

When we're traumatized, we may feel as if we're bewildered and in a daze. We may realize, *I have never felt this way before.* We may also be convinced that life is now truly dangerous: *I am so scared that only horrible things will happen.* We often cannot think clearly or even move; it's as if our feet are permanently stuck in concrete. Sometimes we feel helpless or apathetic about our ability to do anything that will help resolve the crisis. Yet almost always we feel a sense of urgency, as if some type of action needs to take place now, but what? We sometimes feel extreme discomfort with no sense of relief.

I'm aware of these feelings, not only from my own experience, but also as I have worked with people over the years in my counseling profession. I have advised people walking through depression, affairs, divorce, past abortions, disease, sexual abuse, and grief.

Considering that people in crisis feel an intense range of emotions that can change at a moment's notice, how do we walk with someone undergoing a severe trial and do it well? Sometimes we give up, feeling as if we cannot really make a difference. Sometimes we walk with a friend who is so needy we quickly realize we can't possibly meet all the needs she has. Some of us are so busy we don't take the time to reach out in meaningful ways. Oh, has God convicted me in this area! As I look back over my life, I see now that I have passed up many opportunities to love someone in crisis. So often I didn't write the note or bring the meal or come to visit with a hug or a flower. I tear up just thinking about that as I write. What does the grown-up girlfriend do for a friend in crisis so that at the end of the day, when she crawls into bed, she hears her Savior saying, *Well done, My good and faithful servant. I am well pleased at how your heart lifted up your friend today*?

GOING THROUGH CRISIS (YOUR OWN)

Figuring out how you respond to crisis is a good starting point when trying to understand how to walk through crisis with someone else. Many of us don't go through crisis with our friend well because we don't do crisis in our own lives well! We may even deny that we have a crisis or try to deal with our own crisis by taking care of everyone else. So think about any crises you've experienced firsthand. What was your response to them? Were you able to connect with God and others?

I have discovered some valuable insights into myself through my own crisis. To admit aloud that I need anything is difficult for me. My fear is that nobody will sign up to help with those needs, so I won't ask, thereby avoiding the rejection. I'm sure this comes from all sorts of roots—growing up as the independent middle child in a family that didn't often signal our needs to each other, as well as being rejected by a friend and not wanting to risk that feeling again. Yet the bottom line is that I am still responsible to function as God asks me to in the midst of crisis. I am to face it, name it, need in it, and learn from it.

Some people deal with crisis in the opposite way from me. They demand too much from people who cannot possibly supply all their needs. These wounded people do not go to God often enough. Still others seem to be in constant crisis—often of their own making.

Since trials are promised to each of us, we need to be prepared to go through difficult times. Growing in our understanding of ourselves and developing healthy female friendships now can help in this preparation. Of course, nothing will prepare us more than developing an intimate walk with the Lord. On the morning after I had been told about the inoperable tumor in my pancreas and the positive lymph node in my neck, I woke early and huddled in a ball on the couch. I called out to Jesus for every ounce of strength that I was going to need to walk this journey. He gave me Psalm 91 that morning: "He who dwells in the shelter of the Most High will rest in the shadow of the Almighty. . . . You will not fear the terror of night, nor the arrow that flies by day. . . . For he will command his angels concerning you to guard you in all your ways." My favorite words of all come in verse 16: "With long life will I satisfy him and show him my salvation." As I read God's truth, I began to feel the peace only He can provide.

Some people struggle with anger at God for allowing crisis in their lives. At some level I understand this anger, but for me the anger would only serve to alienate me from the greatest source of power, strength, grace, love, tenderness, and protection available to me. I had to go to Him from the start to allow Him to hold me. And He has.

Become an expert on your own response in crisis so you will

be prepared when crisis hits you or a dear friend. Discover more about how you deal with crisis by watching how you respond to even the smallest of troubles. Do you get anxious or depressed? Do you jump to conclusions or assume the worst? The more aware you are of your own reactions, the more you can be sensitive to what your friend needs emotionally when she walks through crisis.

GOING THROUGH CRISIS (WITH YOUR FRIEND)

In part, this is a difficult issue to write on. Why? Because each of us is unique. We tend to try to comfort people in ways that we like to be comforted. Going through crisis with another person, however, requires knowing her well. With that in mind, let me offer some general guidelines on how to walk through crisis with another as her grown-up friend. I'll then deal specifically with four common types of crises in women's lives.

In chapter 7, we explained why a woman will only open her heart to a friend if she feels safe—confident that her friend will deal tenderly with her deepest thoughts and feelings. That is why we need to ask ourselves, *Are we safe?* We may need to tell our friend that we want to be a safe place for her and ask her what that would look like. At times this may change, though it usually means listening well, being there physically and verbally, being able to handle even wrong emotions with care. It also means holding out hope for our friend.

Early in my crisis journey, I found some helpful thoughts from author Archibald Hart. I needed to understand hope in fresh and tangible ways, and this quote helped me do that. In fact, it made *hope* the focus of my battle against cancer:

> *There is just one thing you can say to someone who has lost hope: Never give up on hope. I know it sounds paradoxical, but hear me out! No matter how bad the*

situation is or how despairing your circumstances are, you must never NEVER give up hope. Never, never, never. Never give up hope for an ailing partner. Never give up hope for your children. Never give up hope for yourself. Why? Because if you give up on hope, you give up on life itself. If hope dies, you die. As a friend of mine once said, "As long as you keep hope alive, hope will keep you alive."

Why hope when circumstances are hopeless? The answer is simple—because we were created for hope. Our bones were bred for hope. Our lungs can't breathe, our hearts won't beat and our spirits can't thrive without it. God placed us in a world over which we have little control. And as if to compensate for this helplessness, He placed in our souls the capacity to hope—to hope for better times, to dream of better places, to pray for better outcomes, to seek better ways through life. Hope is more than optimism. Optimism is what we generate. Hope is God given, a powerful, spiritual and psychological means for transcending the circumstances. Hebrews 6:19 tells us that Christian hope is a sure and steadfast anchor for the soul. But this hoping comes only as a gift of grace and is powerfully linked to the promises of God. In fact, they are inseparable. Because you believe God's promises you can hope in the future. Without this future, there is nothing to hope in.[1]

Without hope, there will be despair. That's why when we're walking through any crisis with a friend, one of the best things we can do is to gently and tenderly offer the hope we have, being patient until she begins to hope again. Often, you don't even need to use words to do this. I remember the day a month or so after my diagnosis that a friend called to ask me to go boating. She knows that boating is one of my greatest loves—it ranks right up there with riding horses. I got on my slalom ski, which I've had since I was fifteen, and flew through the water as long as I thought my body could. As I did, I sang and let the wind flow in my face. It was a wonderful, hope-renewing day!

Friends have offered me hope in many other tangible ways. One writes my name in red lipstick on her bathroom mirror as a reminder to pray for me every day! Another told me I looked pretty even though I'd just finished a course of chemo treatment and knew I looked as emaciated as if I'd just walked out of a concentration camp.

Be prepared to offer grace to your friend, for this will give you patience when you feel she should be "over" the crisis. As we encourage our friend to hope, we can also encourage her to keep a positive attitude. Attitude has such a huge impact on our daily experiences. When you hear your friend getting negative, perhaps ask her what she is feeling that day. Listen to her. Listening says, "I care and I am here for you." Then try to help her see that while today feels gloomy, there's hope that tomorrow may be different. I've found that on the hard days of my illness, having a friend offer me grace, hope, encouragement, or laughter chased away the worry, fear, and even fatigue, and provided me with a "turnaround moment."

One great way of offering support is by helping your friend understand that she does have some power over her situation. She has the power to make choices, to get up, to get dressed, and to think differently. She can even draw on the supernatural strength that comes from our Lord. Crisis often makes us feel as if we've lost all control, and we forget that we have the power to choose hope and joy over depression, despair, and fear.

Some crises seem to go on and on. Are we prepared to keep walking with our friend and encouraging her to endure? It takes at least a year to work out the feelings that come from a

significant loss—and usually it takes much longer. A death will
be felt for a lifetime, but the goal is to help your friend become
less consumed by the grief.

Fortunately many friends have rallied around me. One set
up a Web site where people can read my journal entries and
prayer requests as I battle this cancer. By spring 2006, almost
17,000 hits had been made on the Web site, almost 400 entries
had been added to my guest book, and 763 e-mails had been
sent. I have saved each of these notes in a file on my computer
as well as in a basket in my bedroom. They remind me of
God's love through the body of Christ. I also have saved every
single card that has been sent to me.

After learning of the diagnosis, friends contacted me from
everywhere, including my hometown and the University of
Nebraska. People made meal after meal, planted my flowers, ran errands, came to chemotherapy with me, cleaned my
house, made me laugh when I needed to laugh, and cried and
held me when I needed to cry and be held. My cell-group
friends organized a prayer time each Monday afternoon, and
we have gathered and prayed not just for me but also for each
other and for God's hand of protection and power over our
lives in the last year.

Even people I don't know have reached out to me. On my
last birthday, two young women sent flowers and a gift card
for my favorite coffeehouse to the home where I was staying
while being treated. I do not even know these young women,
but oh how I love them for their godly love in my life and their
sweet intention of getting that beautiful gift to me.

I have been so humbled by the grown-up friends God has
used to help sustain me through this journey. I weep at times
over the love of people, and I long to love back in the ways
I have been loved. God has taught me much about Himself
through the love of others, and He has taught me how to receive

and how to need, two areas in which I needed some heavy-duty work! No doubt you also have friends who are going through difficult times. I'd like to tell you what I've learned about supporting friends through four difficult situations.

Divorce or Widowhood

Since as many as 50 percent of marriages end in divorce, it's likely that at least one of our friends will divorce or separate from her husband. Others may lose their spouses through death. Obviously, each situation is different, so how we respond will be different as well. We can openly offer our compassion to a friend whose husband has left her or died. That means being a safe, listening friend who asks her often during her journey what her needs are. At times she will want to socialize, and at other times she will not want to be included with all the couples.

Never assume you know what she wants. If she wants to talk about her experience, listen. If you have not walked through a divorce or widowhood, do not act as if you have. Urging her to date is not the answer to her crisis, but do pray for her if she jumps right into dating. Ask her if she wants to hear your heart about that. If you notice she is isolating herself, keep trying to connect. This might test your ability to endure and be patient!

If your friend divorced her husband and you see no biblical reason for her action, you may need to work out some serious issues between the two of you. This process may involve forgiveness and repentance, or it may result in a parting of ways. I would advocate really seeking the Lord and praying through this crisis. This may take some time.

I've frequently seen people who have been divorced or widowed feel such abandonment and rejection. Often, their friends don't intentionally hurt them; they just don't know what to do. Don't abandon a friend going through divorce or grieving for her husband. Be there for her, and continue to invite and include her in social activities.

Sick Child

The son of Barb, one of my dear friends, was diagnosed with diabetes as a toddler. It was a very serious condition. I mentioned to Barb the other day that even though my husband and I took the classes to learn how to do blood sugar checks and insulin shots so we could take care of Matthew at times, I had been clueless about the hurt and fear she felt. I wish I could go back and walk through that crisis with her in a more helpful and present way. I would have been at that hospital more; I would have cried with her more; and I would have asked her about the loneliness of having a child with special needs. Barb still gets up at night to check on Matthew, even though he is now ten years old.

Because we are so busy, it is easy to become self-absorbed and not see our friend's needs, let alone meet them. I have watched a woman in Siloam Springs do a marvelous job caring for her friend, whose young daughter has cerebral palsy. She has taken this girl to classes, babysat her, and gone to classes to learn more. She is truly a grown-up girlfriend to her friend and a wonderful model of how to walk this crisis journey.

By reading about the sickness of a friend's child, you can become an "assistant expert" for her. Listen to your friend when she needs to talk. You could run errands for her at times or help her think through ways to make her own life easier. I had to be talked into getting a house cleaner when I became ill. Even though cleaning my own house was now out of the question, I did not want to break down and call a house cleaner.

Don't be afraid to ask your friend how you could minister to her in meaningful ways. She might have ideas of her own!

Death

Grief and loss take much time to walk through. It can take a long time to really come out on the other side. If we have not lost a loved one, we simply do not know what it feels like. Yet we can still be a friend. We must not push our friend to "get over it." This is a great opportunity and test of our own feelings. Can we feel with her? Can we empathize? She will know if we can or not. If she pulls away, it might be because we are missing her heart.

Meeting her needs at this time is a delicate situation and requires an intentional heart on your part. Chances are your friend has never been through the loss of someone close, so she is figuring out what she needs as she goes. Try to do that with her. Ask her if she would like to talk about her loved one. Send encouraging cards throughout the year of the loss. *Do* acknowledge the anniversary of the loss. This is very meaningful to most people. Most important, stay involved. Feelings of loss do not diminish quickly, even though we all want them to.

In chapter 10, you read a short excerpt written by my friend Cheryl, in which she explained her experience of losing a brother to cancer. Cheryl is an introvert. She has no great need to verbally process her feelings, but she feels deeply. I remember Cheryl being very tired that year. She had little energy for socialization. I so wanted to help her, to console her, to be with her, and yet that was not what she needed. She did need prayer and love, and she needed my shoulder to rest her head on that evening in church. In those moments she knew of my love and I knew of her broken heart, and that was enough.

Illness

Depression, multiple sclerosis, autoimmune problems, and cancer are just a few of the many difficult diseases that can afflict our friends or ourselves. Four years ago my husband was diagnosed with oral cancer again. This time, it was stage 3. He would need hard-core radiation and chemotherapy. I remember trying to figure out how to meet his needs. For some time he was even unable to speak, so communicating was very difficult. In that next year I dealt with the feelings of wondering whether I would spend the rest of my life as a widow.

I did not let people know my feelings. I had decided they could not understand. God had some work to do with me! In fact, most of what I have learned about walking with a friend through illness I learned through the people God brought into my life after the cancer diagnosis.

Earlier I mentioned my church community group and our Monday afternoon prayer times that we started soon after the diagnosis. We have met continually—except for a three-month period I had to spend away from home. One day last fall, they asked, as they often do, "How are you?" That day I just couldn't put my feelings into words or even tell them what I needed. Instead, tears just fell down my cheeks. Rather than acting uncomfortable and moving on to another topic, they gently waited until I could speak. Then they told me to call anytime about anything, especially when I needed prayer. They also told me they'd be over that Sunday afternoon to help me decorate for Christmas. When they left, I felt as if I'd been with Jesus.

Erin Smalley has also modeled what it means to be a grown-up friend. Never once after hearing my diagnosis did she suggest we back out of writing this book. Instead, she said, "We can do it, girl!" She did not lose hope in me and regularly calls and encourages me with her joyful spirit.

FRIENDS ON THE JOURNEY

Crisis throws us into an intense state of loneliness. We may fight it but, oh, how we need people. You may need them differently than I do, but the need to connect is there. I long to do better at walking through crisis with my suffering friends. I want to be a grown-up girlfriend to the women who have traveled from other states to cook and clean for me and to sit on the couch with me. God has used an awful situation to grow my heart and draw me closer to Himself and to others.

Who in her right mind wants to sign up for crisis, tragedy, trauma? I don't know too many who do—myself included! I would much rather be prepared than unprepared for crisis, however. It is a part of life, not so much to be feared but to face with the belief that we will be sustained, whether we walk through it ourselves or with a friend.

The grown-up girlfriend . . .

. . . gently and tenderly offers hope to a friend in crisis, patiently supporting her until she begins to hope again.

. . . .

REFLECTION QUESTIONS

1. What would you say is the most difficult crisis you have faced in your life thus far?

2. What have you learned about walking through crisis, either a friend's or your own?

3. What strengths can you draw on when walking through crises with a friend? Are you safe? Are you a good listener? Do you hang in there and endure? Do you work to understand others' needs?

4. What does hope mean to you?

5. What do you think you have yet to learn about trials and crises in order to be a grown-up girlfriend?

12

THE GROWN-UP FRIEND
PASSES ON WHAT SHE KNOWS

[Erin]

*Let us not give up meeting together, as some
are in the habit of doing, but let us encourage one
another—and all the more as you
see the Day approaching.*
HEBREWS 10:25

*The whole purpose of spiritual direction is to
penetrate beneath the surface of a man's life,
to get behind the facade of conventional gestures
and attitudes which he presents to the world,
and to bring out his inner spiritual freedom,
his inmost truth, which is what we call the
likeness of Christ in his soul.*
THOMAS MERTON

*My friends have made the story of my life.
In a thousand ways they have turned
my limitations into beautiful privileges.*
HELEN KELLER

I will never forget the day when Taylor, then a fifth grader,
came home from school and showed me a paper she had written entitled "My Mom Is My Hero!" I began to panic. I imag-
ined her first sentence might be something like this: "My mom
is my hero for the days she picks me up from school in her

pajamas after she has been at home all day doing laundry and scrubbing toilets." Or maybe she wrote, "My mom is my hero for the way she has a sudden mood swing three-quarters of the way through each month. I am uncertain why she suddenly becomes increasingly impatient with me and my siblings."

However, to my great delight, I noticed—once I had gathered the courage to read her essay—that one of the first things Taylor mentioned was that "my mom is a good friend to many." Truly I was humbled that she might even attach those words to me—even if I am not the perfect friend.

Whether we do it consciously or not, we pass on what we know. Friendship is obviously a critical area of life, so another mark of the grown-up friend is that she passes on what she knows to her own kids—as well as the young women (nieces, neighbors, students, fellow apartment dwellers) all around her. Sometimes this is done formally—perhaps as a mentor (which we'll discuss later in this chapter)—but more often it is done without our even knowing it.

OUR FIRST MENTORS

So how do grown-up girlfriends pass on what they know? First, don't assume that only moms have this privilege. Although a number of the stories in this chapter come from my experiences with my daughters, every woman can be a model for younger women. If you are single or married with no children, the Lord will bring young women into your life who become somewhat like daughters. Think about your close friends' girls, your nieces, the little girls you know at church, or maybe the young coworker who is just starting her career. (Later in this chapter, I'll introduce you to Shanon, a college student I had the privilege of mentoring. Actually, she taught me some things too!) The Lord has a purpose for these relationships. Begin thinking about how He may want to use you in younger gals' lives.

Second, become aware of just how powerful your influence can be. We often do things in life because we have had them modeled for us—intentionally or unintentionally. Shortly after we married, Greg made an interesting observation. In our first year of marriage, we had been to my parents' home in Phoenix and my grandmother's home in North Dakota. I'd also recently set up our first kitchen in our Denver apartment. Greg said, "I am shocked at how many of the same things you and your mom and grandma all have in your kitchens."

I had never really noticed any similarity, so I asked him to tell me what he'd noticed. "Let's see," he said, "you have the same dish towels, the same large white plastic bowls, the same colander to drain our spaghetti noodles, and even the same measuring cups."

He also said he'd noticed we arranged our kitchens similarly. Our spices were in approximately the same location, our towels were all folded neatly in a drawer, and our pots and pans were in the cabinet closest to the oven.

Suddenly, it occurred to me. My mom had never instructed me formally on what kitchen items to purchase and where to keep them. I simply had bought what was familiar to me and what I had seen her use over the years. I assume my mom had done the same thing years ago. Three generations of kitchens—thousands of miles apart—and yet so much alike.

That got me thinking. How many other things was I doing simply because they had been unintentionally modeled for me? Although how I arranged my kitchen wasn't all that critical, I knew I was going about other areas of my life in haphazard ways—doing things I thought I should be doing because of what had been modeled for me.

Within a few years of my conversation with Greg, we

were blessed with two little girls. At that point I realized I'd better sharpen my own convictions because they would become the foundation of our children's beliefs. I also became more concerned that my actions be consistent with my words.

Even today, I struggle with this at times. For instance, many times my kids come running into a room yelling at the top of their voices.

"Maddy hit me!"

"No, Garrison hit me!"

When the screaming escalates, I get pulled into the intensity of it all. I find myself screaming right back at them, "Stop it! You may not scream at each other!"

And I wonder where they get their bad habits from? I can hear my tone and see my posture as they interact angrily with one other. It is a mirror image of me! How ironic that I am punishing them for the exact thing I have taught them.

If you're a mom, you may already be aware of the need to align what you tell your children to do with how you behave. Likewise, if you're a supervisor, you may have learned that your employees are watching you closely. If you expect them to put in a full day's work, they'd better see you putting in at least eight hours each day and calling in sick only when you're legitimately under the weather. But have you ever considered how much you can teach your daughters and other young women in your life how to be Christlike, grown-up girlfriends?

A girl's earliest friendships are a ripe training ground for developing good interpersonal skills. In other words, how she interacts with her first friends may affect how she relates later on to her classmates, teammates, roommates, and spouse. The following skills are especially important to teach girls and young women as they negotiate their friendships:

- conflict resolution
- communication skills
- forgiveness
- self-awareness
- different levels of intimacy

Other important interpersonal skills include:

- boundaries in friendships
- embracing the personality differences of our friends
- letting friendships go
- modeling Christ to our friends
- praying with our friends

How can we go about transferring these skills to the girls and young women in our lives? First, we have to build a foundation of trust and safety within our own relationships with these young ladies. Otherwise, our formal teaching will go in one ear and out the other. That means, of course, modeling the very principles of grown-up friendship we discuss in this book.

As I've became more aware of the impact my modeling has on my own daughters, I've felt more challenged than ever to model love in the midst of being hurt, to offer grace when a friend offends me, to rejoice when my friend is blessed, to offer support to my friend in the midst of trials, to pray for my friendships, and to include Taylor and Maddy in some of the fun activities with my friends. I want to continue to become a better role model to them, simply by letting them watch me within my friendships. I am well aware that I am not a perfect friend, which means that sometimes they see the trials as well as the triumphs.

Not long ago, I had some time alone in the car with my

older daughter, Taylor, who is nearly thirteen and a seventh grader. I was so glad to finally have some time alone with her so she could tell me more about something that had happened to her the previous week. While she'd been back in Missouri visiting some of her old friends, she'd mentioned to me over the phone that she'd run into her old friend Casey at the community pool.

So as we were driving, I casually said, "Tell me what happened last week at the pool when you saw Casey." I knew that she and Casey had had a pretty intense falling-out before we moved, and it was very hurtful to Taylor. We had discussed it several times over the past year, and ultimately I had encouraged Taylor to forgive this little girl in her heart, even though we had moved away.

Unbelievably, one year later Taylor saw Casey face-to-face on her trip to our old town. As she described their encounter, I continued to drive. I was thinking, *This is such a fabulous example of all the teaching we have done with Taylor about friendships*, and I was mentally patting myself on the back.

All of a sudden Taylor screamed at me, "Mom, pull over!" I panicked, thinking maybe she was carsick—but I wasn't so lucky. She had noticed flashing lights following close behind my car—I was being pulled over. Try explaining to a police officer that you were speeding because you were so intent on listening to your preteen describe how she'd run into her friend with whom she'd had a strained relationship for more than a year. ("And to top it off, Officer, I am writing a book on the topic of friendship. . . ." All I can say is this: Pride cometh before the fall!)

I was given a whopping speeding ticket and then, boy, did the mood change in the car. Finally, about ten miles post-ticket, I was able to say, "Taylor, please tell me how it ended." I was blown away by what I heard. Taylor told me she took the initiative and asked Casey if she would forgive her for whatever she might have done to offend her. Casey in return asked Taylor to forgive her. Then they actually had some fun together at the pool.

I began to cry, not only about my ticket, but because of the maturity in my daughter's actions. We had spent so much time discussing friendships and how to handle the hurts that happen in any relationship. Taylor took to heart what she had learned about forgiveness not only from our talks, but also from church, her small group, and other positive influences.

I've also discussed the basket levels of friendships with my girls. They really grabbed hold of that analogy. Early on, however, Maddy used it in a way I hadn't really intended. One night we were sitting at the dinner table, and Maddy, who is definitely the more assertive of the two, shrieked at her sister, "Taylor, if you don't move your elbow off my side of the table, I am going to move you into my basket number fifty-nine."

Of course, Taylor couldn't wait to let her know that there was no such thing as basket number fifty-nine. Never to be beaten, Maddy screamed, "If there was one, *you'd* be in it!"

Fortunately, the girls have applied the basket analogy in more constructive ways since then. I love to ask them, "Who is in your basket number one and why?" Over the years, I sure wish someone had asked me that question. It might have saved me some heartbreaks with girlfriends. I love to challenge them as to why they want to be friends with someone . . . especially an intimate friend.

It has also been a powerful tool to help them become intentional about what they desire in the character of their basket one friendships and to set boundaries with their friends. Occasionally they've realized they need to shift a friend to another basket. I readily remind both of my girls that they are called to *love* others but are not called to *intimacy* with every friend. The Lord reserves deep intimacy for a select few He places in their lives.

I have taken out the stacking baskets I have in my kitchen cupboard to give them a visual of how small basket one really is and how we must become discerning about whom we place in that special basket. Finally, I remind them that Christ must be our first friend—dead center in basket one—so He can guide us and provide love for our relationships.

Most of the instruction on friendship I've given my daughters hasn't come when we sit down for formal discussions, however. It's more likely to happen during a car ride, on a date night together, or when we're sitting poolside—in other words, whenever an opportunity presents itself. Make yourself available to listen and share your own experiences and thoughts. Let the young women in your life know that you are available to talk about friendships and their challenges.

At some point, we must allow girls to spread their wings and discover their own convictions within friendships. We must allow them to discover what works with their personalities and tendencies. This may mean stepping aside and being nothing other than a listening ear in the midst of difficulties. However, letting them know you are available and willing to assist them in working through relational issues is meaningful. Deuteronomy 6:7 reminds us that we are to "teach [God's standards] diligently to your sons [and daughters] and . . . talk of them when you sit in your house and when you walk by the way and when you lie down and when you rise up" (NASB).

Another way we can have a positive influence on these girls' friendships is through prayer. One mom told me she has prayed for years that her daughter, Amanda, would have wisdom in selecting friends. What a great prayer! We can pray for girls in our lives too. Our prayer might be something like this:

Lord, help my daughter [or niece or other young lady] have wisdom when selecting her girlfriends. Please bring girls into her life who love you, most importantly, but who also make good choices in life. Protect her from harm and bless her abundantly with healthy friendships. Amen.

I've spent time praying for and with my daughters about their friendships. I am utterly amazed at what God will do when we ask. When we moved to Arkansas, Taylor left a tight-knit group of friends from great families. She was heartbroken to leave Branson, Missouri, for this reason. I spent many nights on my knees asking for at least one godly friend for Taylor, who was entering middle school. The Lord actually revealed this girl to us through our first meeting with Taylor's new teacher. Mrs. Wilt told us that there was a girl in the class whom Taylor would definitely connect with. She described her as "beautiful inside and out." And wouldn't you know, Taylor and Chanel met on the first day of school and since then have become great friends. God was so faithful to us, and Taylor was able to see what God will do when we pray for friends.

It has now been nearly a year since our move, and God has filled Taylor's baskets abundantly. She has maintained her precious friendships in Branson, but the Lord has responded to our plea for well-rounded baskets of friends in Arkansas. If you or your child is experiencing a season of loneliness due to a move or maybe just "life," spend time asking the Lord to fill that vacancy right now. I have watched Him answer that prayer again and again in my own life and my kids' lives.

BECOMING A MENTOR — WHO, ME?

Job Title: *Mentor*

Wanted: *Imperfect woman (who must be seeking God's will in her own life) to spend time with a younger woman. She must be willing to work long hours praying, offering continual unconditional love, and seeking God's purpose in her relationship with this younger woman.*

She must offer friendship, companionship, and encouragement—even if the outcome looks bleak. She must also be willing to share what the Lord has taught her over her lifetime—including what He has taught her through her female friends. She must be able to laugh, cry, and love— even when the younger woman is feeling unlovable.

Compensation: *Great blessings on a daily basis.*

Okay, so want ads for a formal mentor don't really exist. However, if they did, they might read something like the fictitious ad above. So what is mentoring? It is a relationship in which one person empowers another by sharing her experiences, gifts, and time. The key to mentoring is realizing that God has given each of us experiences and knowledge to share with other women. He knows who we should be passing on our wisdom to—we just need to ask for His leading so we don't miss a golden opportunity to impact another woman.

Informal Mentors

You may be approached by a woman seeking mentoring because of a personal need—she might desire to grow spiritually or professionally or become a better mother. Many of my greatest mentors have come in the form of my grown-up girlfriends.

Recently I went to a women's conference with a group of my friends. As we sat around the table discussing parenting, marriage, spiritual struggles, and other lighter topics, I realized how invaluable the feedback, validation, encouragement, wisdom, and discernment I receive from my girlfriends is.

My first Bible study group years ago was filled with women who informally mentored me. Greg and I had just moved to Los Angeles. I was a brand-new mom and had no idea what to expect staying home with a baby. A neighbor encouraged me to come with her to a luncheon where the women would be placed into Bible study groups. I held my six-week-old daughter closely and sat nervously as I looked around a room of strange faces.

A sweet, older lady approached me and insisted I join her group—she let me know I would "fit in just perfectly." The following week I showed up at Inez's group. We sat around a horseshoe-shaped table to study the Word of God and memorize Scripture together. I had no idea the impact these ladies would have on me. We closed each study by sharing our hearts with each other, and I received invaluable feedback from that group. They loved me through my first years of motherhood. In essence, they were my first mothering mentors.

The first time my sweet baby, Taylor—who had grown into a usually sweet toddler—threw a temper tantrum at the grocery store, I was devastated. I went to the next Bible study feeling like a total failure as a mother. I needed advice on how to handle this situation the next time. These women understood my feeling like a "horrible mother" and assured me they had all been there before. They didn't stop there, however. Inez, our leader, talked about how children have free will and a sin nature. She assured me that Taylor's throwing a temper tantrum had less to do with me and more to do with Taylor's fallen nature. One by one the other ladies told me how they had dealt with their children in public when they threw temper tantrums. I left feeling so much better and had practical tools to use. The great thing about this group was that each week someone new seemed to be dealing with a major issue. In essence, we took turns mentoring each other.

Then there was my "cooking mentor," Susan, who was also a dear friend. I always wanted to become a good cook, but it just didn't happen. I was even anxious about going to the grocery store when I was first married. I had spent little time in the kitchen growing up and now was expected to feed my husband. Several years into my marriage, I was blessed to meet Susan, who was a caterer. When we spent time together, she was often preparing food to deliver to an event. I savored my time with her since I learned so much just by watching her. She even helped me prepare the meal for my son's dedication day. I think Greg was extremely grateful for this friend as well—we finally had something to eat besides macaroni and cheese and frozen pizza!

Formal Mentors

Initially it was hard for me to wear the formal mentor hat—especially outside of my own home. I knew I could wear the mother hat; however, it was a step outside my comfort zone the first time I committed to formally mentor a young lady.

We had just moved to Branson. Our new home was next to a ministry that sought mentors for the college-age women who worked there. A mutual friend encouraged Shanon and I to get to know each other and possibly form a mentor/mentee relationship. Before I knew it, Shanon was knocking on my door. We hit it off immediately. Shanon and I met over the next two years and spent time talking and praying. We discovered we both loved to run, although she was a bit faster and stronger than I was—seeing as I was the older woman in the relationship.

The first time Shanon and I met, we talked about the specific areas of life in which she felt I could encourage her. One primary thing she desired to do was gain further insight and understanding into who she truly was in Christ. She also wanted to better understand her core fears, reactions, and personality tendencies. She also talked about a desire to pray more and spend more time in the Word.

We met once a week for one hour, and often that one hour turned into two. However, she was aware of my hectic schedule and understood if I had to reschedule or leave to pick up my kids. We always began our time with prayer and then covered our reading material if we had agreed on a specific reading assignment. (We read through several books together.) We talked about how the reading applied to each of us and how it had impacted us. Our time always ended by my checking in on several areas in which she'd asked for accountability, and then I prayed for her specific requests.

I almost always left our times together encouraged. Although our relationship was set up as a formal mentor relationship, Shanon became a dear friend to me as well. She encouraged me and prayed with me through some challenging times.

One of my fondest memories of our two years together was sitting at my kitchen table praying for a godly mate for Shanon. Eventually Shanon moved to Texas, and then I moved to Arkansas. I was thrilled and overjoyed when I received "the call" from Shanon earlier this year. She had met the man she was going to marry and had become engaged to him the previous week. I cried as I listened to her excitement over her upcoming marriage. The memories flooded back as we realized how the Lord had answered the many "kitchen table prayers" we had offered up.

I encourage you to begin asking the Lord to lead you to another woman who is a few steps behind you in life or who is currently in a difficult situation. We are all capable of mentoring in one way or another. It may be formal or informal—but be on the lookout for someone God has placed in your path.

Next, seek His purpose in the relationship. He may very well desire you to pass on information and wisdom or to journey with one of His children.

If you are considering beginning a formal mentoring relationship like the one I had with Shanon, you may find the following guidelines helpful:

- See if your church has a mentoring ministry. Seek any helpful resources on mentoring you might be able to find.
- Remember that you cannot give what you do not have. Essentially, you must give out of the overflow of your own life. You must maintain a right relationship with the Lord through consistent Bible study, prayer, confession, and worship.
- Once you've agreed to mentor a young woman, set a date for your meeting. Choose a time and a place that is comfortable for both of you. Remember that the environment needs to be conducive to sharing private information and praying.
- Pray before you meet with your mentee. Allow the Holy Spirit to speak to you and guide your words and actions.
- During your first meeting together, talk together about what areas you and your mentee would like to focus on. Seek the Lord and ask Him what He desires as well.
- You may want to determine the time frame of your relationship—whether you'll meet for one year or one season. At a minimum, set a time to reevaluate whether you both desire to continue meeting together.
- Seek to understand her key struggles. Ask questions about the different seasons of her life or what her biggest hurdles have been.
- If you are reading a book or doing a Bible study together, always come with your lesson prepared.

Mentoring is not always easy, but the Lord delights when we are willing to reach out beyond our comfort zones, and as a result He will bless us with true joy—His joy!

Carrie has served as my informal mentor over the years. She views our relationship as being "fellow journeyers." And truly, that is what being a mentor is: sharing the journey that the Lord has laid before both of you within the relationship. Life experience is a precious gift to share with another woman. The blessings the Lord gives through these opportunities are immeasurable.

The grown-up girlfriend . . .

. . . teaches younger women by modeling love in the midst of hurt, offering support in the midst of trials, praying for her friendships, and occasionally including these younger women in fun activities with her friends.

. . . .

REFLECTION QUESTIONS

1. Think about the women in your life who have served as formal and informal mentors. What impact have these relationships had on you?

2. Spend some time thinking about how you have served as a mentor for other women—either intentionally or not. What relationships come to mind, and how did each of you benefit from the other's influence?

3. Is there currently a younger woman whom you have felt led to reach out to? What could you do today to begin connecting with her? Is there anything specific that has kept you from reaching out to younger women in the past?

13

THE GROWN-UP FRIENDSHIP REQUIRES US TO GROW UP!

[Erin]

*All right believing in God is visibly reflected
in right behavior towards men.*
GEOFFRY B. WILSON

*In the same way, let your light shine before men,
that they may see your good deeds and
praise your Father in heaven.*
MATTHEW 5:16

My senior year of high school in Phoenix was "dreamy." I got out of classes by noon each day, and then typically my friend Jessica and I would go out to lunch at a fast-food place before making the dramatic, life-changing decision about whose house we should go to. We would lie out by the pool at my house, drinking pineapple juice with little umbrellas poking out of the glass, or we'd go to Jessica's and just hang out, watching whatever television show struck our fancy that day.

The other difficult decision was whose car to drive home from school—my 1972 Honda Civic or Jessica's Datsun B210. Sometimes that decision was made for us: My car was so little that, as a prank, a couple of high school guys would sometimes pick it up and place it across a parking spot between two cars.

So when my car was "unavailable," we'd take Jessica's orange Datsun, which often backfired as we drove it out of the parking lot. Off we'd go for our stressful afternoon—television, pool relaxation, and most important, deep conversation. Sometimes we'd actually have to go to our jobs for four hours later in the day—but not until our fun was done. We often said, "I don't want to grow up—let's just stay seniors in high school forever!"

Actually, this desire to keep things comfortable is what many of us strive for in our friendships. Although we don't say it, sometimes we fear what "growing up" in our friendships would mean. Often we think that it might take too much work and effort! We don't mind that our friendships aren't all that they could be—because they are good enough. We don't desire to change a thing because we're comfortable where we are. Change is hard, but I encourage you to seriously contemplate how you could become a grown-up friend. The rewards are many.

Jessica and I thought that life back in 1986 was great. We didn't want to move beyond it, but we had no idea the fullness that life had to offer after high school. We also were unaware of the challenges that were down the road for each of us.

When spring rolled around and graduation neared, Jessica and I had a lot of decisions to make. Should we pursue college or work full-time? Once we chose college, which one should we attend? Should we live at home or in a dorm room?

As you come to the last chapter of this book, you have some big decisions to make as well. Will you choose to become a grown-up friend? What insights from this book could you use to improve your friendships?

Personally, I have thoroughly enjoyed embarking on this journey with you. It began more than five years ago in that Sam's Club parking lot, and it is not finished yet. I'm still discovering what the Lord has to teach me through the relationships that He brings into my life. I know that there is more beyond "graduation." As I approach my twenty-year high school reunion, I am in awe of what the Lord has done in my life since Jessica and I hung out by the pool. I pray that in twenty years, you will look back and see reading this book as a turning point—the beginning of your journey to becoming a grown-up friend.

WHAT DOES GROWING UP REQUIRE?

I'm convinced that being a grown-up friend is not possible unless we choose to grow in Christ and mature in Him. We say that we want to be conformed into His image, but are we a piece of humble clay for Him to mold? We know that at times our clay can get hard and stubborn. Staying comfortable often is our first priority, and becoming godly isn't always comfortable. Christ will bring us what we need for the journey—if we choose to follow Him. The rewards are countless, as we will not only become better friends to others and ourselves, but also better mothers, wives, coworkers, sisters, daughters, and aunts. The impact is endless.

Just see what Scripture has to say:

> No prolonged infancies among us, please. We'll not tolerate babes in the woods, small children who are an easy mark for imposters. God wants us to grow up, to know the whole truth and tell it in love—like Christ in everything. We take our lead from Christ, who is the source of everything we do. He keeps us in step with each other. His very breath and blood flow through us, nourishing us so that we will grow up healthy in God, robust in love.
>
> EPHESIANS 4: 14-16, THE MESSAGE

> *Stop thinking like children. In regard to evil be infants, but in your thinking be adults.*
>
> 1 Corinthians 14:20

Note the emphasis on shifting from our old self-centered thinking to other-centered thinking. As Rick Warren wrote, "Children only think of themselves; grown-ups think of others. God commands, 'Don't think only about your own affairs, but be interested in others, too.'"[1] Clearly Jessica and I had no concerns beyond our own needs and comfort. Oh, how that has changed.

My daughter Maddy modeled this for me at the ripe old age of three as we were packing the car for a trip to Disney World. I don't know about yours, but my house is chaotic when trying to get everything and everyone packed and into the car for the drive to the airport. I typically cannot make it to the car without sweat beading across my forehead.

We were finally all in the car—or so we thought—until we looked back to find that Maddy wasn't in her car seat. Greg began honking the horn until our daughter flew out the door leading into our garage. She had something clutched in her little hand. When she got close enough to Greg's window for us to identify it, our greatest fears were confirmed. It was Gracie, the praying bunny. Greg and I looked at each other in a panic. How in the world could we have forgotten?

You see, Gracie was Maddy's most prized possession. She carried Gracie everywhere and did everything with this stuffed toy. We set a place for Gracie at dinner. She slept with Maddy, she went to church with us, and she even went in Maddy's backpack to preschool. The only problem with having a such a close "friend" was that when Maddy misplaced Gracie, we were witnesses to a complete and total meltdown. It was not fun, and we definitely didn't want to experience it on our vacation.

So Greg tried to convince Maddy that she needed to leave Gracie home. This was no easy task, even though he has a doctoral degree in psychology. Greg attempted to "influence" Maddy by telling her that there were new weight limits on how much luggage we could have and that Gracie would put us over the limit. He instructed Maddy to go put Gracie back up on her bed and let her stay home to watch the house for us while we were gone.* So Maddy hung her head and slowly headed back up the stairs into the house to leave her precious Gracie on her bed. Then we began to wait again . . . and wait and wait.

After several minutes—which felt like hours—Greg began honking again. Before long we saw the door fly open and Maddy reappear. With Gracie in tow. She marched right up to Greg's driver's side window and looked right into his eyes. She said, "Daddy, is Disney World going to be fun?"

Hoping to convince her to obey and get into the car, Greg said, "Yes, Maddy, it is the greatest place on earth. We are going to have the time of our lives. Now just leave Gracie there on the stairs and let's go!"

Maddy hesitated and then said, "Daddy, if Disney World is going to be that fun . . . I want Gracie to go and I'll stay here and watch the house!" I wanted to laugh out loud in an "I told you so" manner, but instead I put on my "curious" face, wondering how in the world Greg would get out of this one. I was proud of what he did next. He opened his door, grabbed Maddy and Gracie into his arms, and placed them in the backseat of our van. He strapped in both girls (Maddy and Gracie), and off we went on our dream vacation.

Grown-up friends are willing to lay down thoughts, feelings,

---

*A woman approached me after I told this story at a speaking engagement to let me know that Greg had told a white lie. I am well aware that he did, and believe me, I've tried to convince Greg that this wasn't a good idea. I just keep praying for him!

and needs at the foot of the cross, believing only Christ can fill us fully. This is exactly what Maddy displayed for me that fateful day. She showed me that she was willing to offer her space on a dream vacation to her best friend. She showed other-centered thinking.

When we allow the Lord to fill us up, we can give to our friends out of His abundance. Of course, as we attempt to serve others, we should keep two things in mind. First, we should not be a doormat to our friends; we can't love and respect others until we love and respect ourselves. On the other extreme, we must be careful to serve others out of love for them and Christ, not for our own selfish purposes.

When we allow Christ to fill us, mold us, and change us, we don't have to use, manipulate, or get angry with friends when they don't give us what we want. Instead, we first grow up in Him so that we can become grown-up friends.

WHAT OTHER CHARACTERISTICS DOES A GROWN-UP FRIEND DISPLAY?

Grown-up friends bring hope, encouragement, love, grace, and truth to others. They lead us as role models and mentors into becoming more Christlike in our relationships. They are often the friends with whom we feel safest and whom we call when we have trauma in our lives. They often function as therapists—though they refuse any payment other than the satisfaction of launching us further down the road.

Ultimately, a grown-up friend brings us to Christ. My sister in Christ Barb went through a very dark season in her marriage. Her story is a testimony and example of what can happen when grown-up friends rally around a friend and do what they do best—encourage their hurting sister to turn toward Him and continue in her journey of becoming grown up. Here's Barb's story, in her own words:

Friends who truly look out for your best, and not what appears "good for you at the moment," are essential in life. I am so grateful that in hard seasons I have had women around me who don't allow me to settle for the easy road but who seek out truth and encourage the desires of my heart, which are excellence and godliness, even when the journey is hard.

It is so much easier to walk through the muck of life when you've got a friend holding out hope for you—and a hand when needed. A nonnegotiable in my closest friendships is that we are truthful and provide a safe place to share the joys and burdens of life. What good is it to pretend that life is all roses when pain may be on every side? Life brings unexpected curves and corners, which can bring fear and anxiety. A basket number one friend is critical during these hours.

For me, such a season came when my husband was involved in an extramarital affair. I asked my girlfriends not to become entangled by anything I might share with them—about the pain I was experiencing or the fear I was feeling. I asked them to hold my bar high and to remind me of a God much stronger than myself. A healer much greater than me. A provider, a sustainer, a redeemer who could transform all things and make them new.

I asked them to help sustain the "breath of life" in my marriage, when the blows of life were calling for a ventilator. I asked them to remind me who my husband really was—a godly man who was making a very ungodly decision. I asked my basket number one friends not to waver in encouraging me; to comfort me moment by moment, but to remind me that it would be the power of God that would bring my husband around.

I asked them to remind me to slow down if I wanted to make a decision in haste. I wasn't in a physically abusive marriage, so time and decisions didn't have to be made immediately. "Let's give the Lord time to work," one friend would always say. My girlfriends prayed for me unceasingly. We still reflect on those "beyond midnight moments," when we all cried out to God to come, heal, and restore. I remember that even though my season was painfully difficult, I felt utter strength! In our "marriage wilderness" I am so grateful that I had friendships in my life who caused me to be spurred on toward excellence.

My mentor always asked me if I had enough strength to get through the day—that day. Looking toward tomorrow's unknown appeared overwhelming; looking back on yesterday was too painful. But each day God was faithful, giving me enough faith for the day! His "manna" for each moment was enough for the day before me.

I remember asking my girlfriends to hold my bar high without wavering unless I whispered the words, "I am down for the count" to them. It was my code meaning "I have no fight left in me." That's when I would need all their support, because it would mean I was getting out of the marriage. I told them they would never hear those words unless I truly felt God's release. Thankfully, I never mumbled those words—although at times I wanted to.

It has been nine years since our marriage wilderness— we'll be celebrating fifteen years of marriage this year with our four beautiful children (two added since that time), and our relationship is stronger than ever. I am so grateful that we fought the fight.

I want God's best, and sometimes that requires walking through a fire, navigating through a valley, or enduring for a season—but the promise of being in His land is the *desire of my heart. I do not want to settle for anything less. Choices such as this are hard to stick with unless you have committed friends who spur you on toward excellence.*

As women we need to give our inner circle of friends permission to say, "Don't let me fall—fight for me when I am weak. Help me run this race with endurance. Tie my shoes when they come untied, and give me water when I am thirsty. Raise my bar when I am lowering it and shout for me on the sidelines to run the race set out before me." That way we might have a flourishing finish and hear God say, "Well done, good and faithful servant."

The wonderful thing is that God doesn't leave us alone to travel the road of becoming grown up. We can walk it with other fellow travelers—our female friends. He can use each of us in our friends' lives in a mighty way. Our female friends can root us on in our seasons of challenge—much as He did in Barb's life.

ARE WE CHOOSING TO GROW UP?

Growing up is a choice, one the Lord lets us make freely. He desires for us to move beyond our preschool days in Him and move on to maturity. "So come on, let's leave the preschool fingerpainting exercises on Christ and get on with the grand work of art. Grow up in Christ" (Hebrews 6:1, *THE MESSAGE*).

Throughout this book, we have discussed what being a grown-up friend requires. It begins by recognizing that we were created for intimacy—specifically with other women— and also identifying the purpose God has for every friendship. A grown-up friend recognizes that there are different levels of intimacy and that not all friends will end up being basket one friends. A grown-up friend works to know herself—particularly her fears, reactions, and coping mechanisms. She knows she'll never be perfect, but she desires to understand her fear buttons and learn to respond instead of reacting. She also sets appropriate boundaries and embraces differences between herself and her friends. She chooses to communicate as a grown-up by becoming aware of what it really means to be a safe friend. She forgives freely and offers grace when necessary. At the same time, she recognizes that friendships can become destructive and that at times she may need to let go of a friendship.

How can you tell if you've become a grown-up friend?

- You accept rather than judge.
- You express your feelings and encourage your friend to do likewise.
- You take responsibility for your feelings and never lay guilt trips on your friend for how you feel.
- You show empathy, compassion, and understanding for her feelings.

You are sensitive to her feelings and needs, but you do not drain yourself by feeling responsible for meeting them. You recognize that each person is responsible for her own feelings, so your friend does not become burdensome to you.

- You do not blame her or attack her, so she does not need to feel defensive or to counterattack.
- You do not advise her or tell her what to do, since you know that this will foster dependency, rob her of the chance to grow, and possibly create resentment later on.
- You are honest with her, even when what you have to say is unpleasant for her, because (a) you respect her

enough to honor her with the truth, (b) you want her to
grow through awareness, and (c) you trust her enough to
manage her own responses.

- When you communicate concerns, you express them
  as statements of your feelings, not as attacks on her
  character.

In *The Road to Daybreak*, Henri Nouwen offers wonderful
insights into what this looks like practically. He says:

> *I learned afresh that friendship requires a constant
> willingness to forgive each other for not being Christ
> and a willingness to ask Christ himself to be the true
> center. When Christ does not mediate a relationship,
> that relationship easily becomes demanding, manipulat-
> ing, oppressive, an arena for many forms of rejection.
> An unmediated friendship cannot last long; you simply
> expect too much of the other and cannot offer the other
> the space he or she needs to grow. Friendship requires
> closeness, affection, support, and mutual encouragement,
> but also distance, space to grow, freedom to be different,
> and solitude. To nurture both aspects of a relationship,
> we must experience a deeper and more lasting affirmation
> than any human relationship can offer.*[2]

Becoming grown up is a lifelong process, and one of the
primary ways we know that it is happening is who we are in
our relationships. So often our pain, sorrow, pride, fears, and
wounds drive us. We end up approaching relationships in one
of two ways: We fill our lives with people and work hard to get
them to meet our needs, or we isolate ourselves and don't really
seek friends. As a result, we are pleasant to our friends but not
committed to finding God's purpose for our friendships—not

just with our casual friends (basket two or three) but even with those close friends to whom we are especially committed (basket one). Honestly, Carrie and I know it can be easier at times not to pursue relationships because of our busyness, insecurities, and fears (such as the fear of being rejected, controlled, or abandoned). Fortunately, God has not allowed us to stay in that place. He has either changed our physical circumstances or our emotional circumstances—by changing and healing our hearts. It can be difficult when we are "gently" pushed to higher ground by our heavenly Father; however, when we see that Christ has called us to be grown up in Him, we neither need to cling to people nor isolate from them.

Here is the really hard part of being grown up: It does not protect us from being hurt. When we are committed to people, there will be wounds. It is part of being human. Growing up helps us to take more and more of those wounds to Christ and allow Him to heal our hearts. This tends to be the easier part of the equation. If we're grown-up friends, we also desire to know what part we've played in producing hurt and pain. It is often easier to see the other party's responsibility loud and clear and not notice what we contributed. However, growing up means we acknowledge our own faults and are willing to change what we have control of—ourselves!

No doubt as you develop into a grown-up friend, you'll experience the great joys and blessings as well as the great sorrows that come with intimate friendship—sometimes in the same relationship. At times it doesn't feel good, and oh, what a loss and grieving process it can be when a friend walks away from you. However, the blessings that friends bring to your life are abundant and well worth any discomfort.

So we encourage you to press on, dear sister in Christ. Press on toward becoming like Christ in your friendships. Press on because it is the healthiest thing you can do. God will smile upon you and bless you as you grow in Him and continue to strive to become a grown-up friend.

The grown-up girlfriend . . .

. . . joyfully travels the path to maturity in the company of her friends.

. . . .

REFLECTION QUESTIONS

1. Where are you in your journey of becoming a grown-up friend? Is anything holding you back? How would you most like to grow?

2. Which are you more likely to do: work hard to get your friends to meet your needs or isolate yourself and avoid seeking new friends?

3. What is the current state of your relationship with the Lord? with your friends?

4. How has this book impacted you personally and/or your friendships?

Notes

Introduction
1. Henri Nouwen, *The Inner Voice of Love* (New York: Random House, 1996), 4.

Chapter 1
1. S. E. Taylor et al., "Biobehavioral Responses to Stress in Females: Tend-and-Befriend, Not Fight-or-Flight," *Psychological Review* 107, no. 3 (2002): 411–429.
2. Jan Yager, *Friendshifts* (New York: Simon and Schuster, 1999), 3–5.
3. Ann Hibbard's book *Treasured Friends* (Grand Rapids: Baker Books, 2004) has also contributed to my appreciation of the benefits of friendship.
4. *Merriam-Webster* online, http://www.merriamwebster.com.

Chapter 2
1. Kass P. Dotterweich and John D. Perry, *Friendship Therapy* (St. Meinrad, Ind.: Abbey Press, 1994).
2. Cathy Lynn Grossman, "Starbucks Stirs Things Up with a God Quote on Cups," *USA Today* (October 19, 2005).

Chapter 3
1. Leslie Parrott, *If You Ever Needed Friends, It's Now* (Grand Rapids: Zondervan, 2000), 18.
2. Matthew Kelly, *The Seven Levels of Intimacy* (New York: Beacon Publishing, 2005), 113–116.
3. Karol Ladd and Terry Ann Kelly mention the three levels of friendship—acquaintances, good friends, and soul mates—in their book, *The Power of a Positive Friend* (West Monroe, La.: Howard Publishing, 2004). I drew on their book while further developing the friendship basket concept. Leslie Parrott's book *If You Ever Needed Friends, It's Now* helped me determine a range for the number of friends each of us has at various levels of intimacy.
4. Hibbard, *Treasured Friends*, 33.
5. Ladd and Kelly, *The Power of a Positive Friend*, 31.

Chapter 4

1. *NIV Life Application Study Bible,* dictionary/concordance (Carol Stream, Ill.: Tyndale House, 2005), 2, 335.
2. Two books that I've found provide a helpful discussion on the heart and the many biblical references to it are *Waking the Dead*, by John Eldredge, and *The DNA of Relationships for Couples*, by Greg Smalley and Robert Paul.
3. From chapter 5, "The Rescue of the Tin Woodman," in *The Wonderful Wizard of Oz* by L. Frank Baum, published in 1900.
4. Our discussion of the Fear Dance has been adapted from *The DNA of Relationships* by Gary Smalley (Carol Stream, Ill.: Tyndale House, 2004). Used with permission.
5. Adapted from Smalley, *The DNA of Relationships.*

Chapter 5

1. Nouwen, *The Inner Voice of Love,* 85.
2. Ibid., 9–10.

Chapter 6

1. William and Patricia Coleman, *Because We're Friends* (Ann Arbor, Mich.: Servant Publications, 1997), 40.
2. Ibid., 64.
3. One useful and well-researched personality preference assessment is the Myers-Briggs Type Indicator. A practical book that explains and applies Myers-Briggs is *Lifetypes* by Sandra Krebs Hirsh and Jean Kummerow (Warner Books, 1989).
4. Michael P. Nichols, *Trust* (New York: Guilford Press, 1996), 101.

Chapter 7

1. Carol Tavris, *The Mismeasure of Woman* (New York: Simon & Schuster, 1992), 198–200. See also Helen Fisher, *Why We Love* (New York: Henry Holt and Company, 2004).
2. Robin Dunbar, *Human Nature* 8, no. 3: 231–246.
3. Sadie F. Dingfelder, "Whispers as Weapons," *Monitor on Psychology* (April 2006), 62–63.
4. Les and Leslie Parrott, *A Good Friend* (Ann Arbor, Mich.: Servant Publications, 1998), 67.
5. Ladd and Kelly, *The Power of a Positive Friend*, 219–227.
6. *Webster's Pocket Dictionary* (Naples, Fla.: Trident Press International), 1997.
7. These four steps are adapted from *The Marriage You've Always Dreamed Of* by Greg Smalley (Carol Stream, Ill.: Tyndale House, 2005), 152–155.

Chapter 8

1. Nichols, *Trust*, 14.
2. "Untitled Hymn (Come to Jesus)" from *Run the Earth, Watch the Sky* (Rocketown Records/DRA, 2003).
3. Everett Worthington, *Handbook of Forgiveness* (Downers Grove, Ill.: InterVarsity Press, revised edition 2003).
4. Ibid., 99.
5. Everett Worthingon, *Forgiving and Reconciling: Bridges to Wholeness and Hope* (Downers Grove, Ill.: InterVarsity Press, 2003), 41.

Chapter 9

1. This definition is a bit of a hybrid. I read the definition on the online *Merriam-Webster* dictionary and then adapted it slightly.
2. Susan Forward, *Emotional Blackmail* (New York: HarperCollins, 1997), 4–6.
3. Jan Yager, *When Friendship Hurts: How to Deal with Friends Who Betray, Abandon, or Wound You* (New York: Fireside, 2002), 30–53.
4. Nouwen, *The Inner Voice of Love*, xvii.

Chapter 10

1. Coleman, *Because We're Friends*, 133.

Chapter 11

1. Archibald Hart, "When We Lose Hope," *Pass It On* newsletter (produced by the American Association of Christian Counselors). Reprinted with permission.

Chapter 13

1. Rick Warren, *The Purpose-Driven Life* (Grand Rapids: Zondervan, 2002), 299. The Scripture in this quote comes from Philippians 2:4.
2. Henri Nouwen, *The Road to Daybreak* (New York: Image Books, 1990), 65.

*A*BOUT THE AUTHORS

ERIN SMALLEY holds a master's degree in clinical psychology and enjoys working with her husband, Greg, writing and speaking on marital and parenting issues. Erin has published numerous articles for *ParentLife, HomeLife,* and *Marriage Partnership* magazines. The Smalleys reside in Siloam Springs, Arkansas, with their two daughters, Taylor and Maddy, and their son, Garrison.

CARRIE OLIVER is the directory of the University Relationships Initiative at the Center for Relationship Enrichment at John Brown University and has a private practice as a counselor. Carrie is a speaker at national conferences and women's retreats and travels with her husband, Gary, leading marriage enrichment seminars and parenting workshops. Carrie cowrote the book *Raising Sons and Loving It!* with her husband, and she also coauthors a "Couple Counsel" column in Marriage Partnership magazine.

ERIN SMALLEY
Smalley Relationship Center
1482 Lakeshore Drive
Branson, MO 65616
800-84-TODAY (86329)
Fax: 417-336-3515
E-mail: murphysmalley@aim.com
Web site: www.smalleyonline.com

CARRIE OLIVER
The Center for Relationship Enrichment
200 W. University St.
Siloam Springs, AR 72761
Fax: 479-524-7373

LOOK FOR THESE ADDITIONAL RELATIONSHIP RESOURCES WHEREVER FINE BOOKS ARE SOLD:

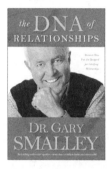

THE DNA OF RELATIONSHIPS
by Dr. Gary Smalley

Have you ever felt as if you're repeating the same mistakes in your relationships? Dr. Gary Smalley tells you the whys and hows of relationships.

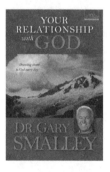

YOUR RELATIONSHIP WITH GOD
by Dr. Gary Smalley

In this book, Gary reveals how the stresses and busyness of life distracted him from his relationship with God. Through a series of difficult and life-threatening circumstances, God got Gary's attention, and now he enjoys a vital and refreshing relationship with God. In this book, Gary gives you six daily habits God taught him during these trials in order to stay grounded and rejuvenated.

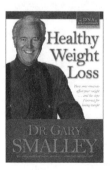

HEALTHY WEIGHT LOSS
by Dr. Gary Smalley

Weight and relationships are intricately intertwined. How we eat affects our relationships, and how we relate to our loved ones affects how we eat. Often weight-loss diets ignore the key relational dynamic that helps keep people motivated to practice healthy eating habits. In this book, you'll learn how to lose weight in a holistic way.

MEN'S RELATIONAL TOOLBOX
by Dr. Gary Smalley, Dr. Greg Smalley, and Michael Smalley

Men understand the world in a unique way—and they approach relationships in a special way as well. This book is designed to help guys figure out the nuts and bolts of satisfying relationships—both at work and at home.

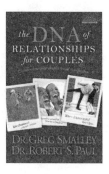

THE DNA OF RELATIONSHIPS FOR COUPLES
by Dr. Greg Smalley and Dr. Robert Paul

Through the stories of four fictionalized couples, Greg Smalley and Robert Paul help readers understand how to work at correcting dangerous relationship habits. The lives of the couples depicted in the book illustrate how to break the fear dance, create safety in a relationship, listen to each other's emotions, and much more. This book is a unique relationship book that uses stories to demonstrate what real relationship change looks like.

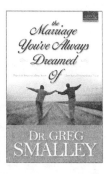

THE MARRIAGE YOU'VE ALWAYS DREAMED OF
by Dr. Greg Smalley

Discover what the marriage you've always dreamed of looks like. Find out how to transform marriage problems into opportunities to love each other—how to look for treasures in the trials. Discover how to experience God's best for your marriage.

DON'T DATE NAKED
by Michael and Amy Smalley

Straight talk to single guys and girls on what healthy relationships look like.

FOCUS ON THE FAMILY®

Welcome to the family!

Whether you purchased this book, borrowed it, or received it as a gift, we're glad you're reading it. It's just one of the many helpful, encouraging, and biblically based resources produced by Focus on the Family for people in all stages of life.

Focus began in 1977 with the vision of one man, Dr. James Dobson, a licensed psychologist and author of numerous best-selling books on marriage, parenting, and family. Alarmed by the societal, political, and economic pressures that were threatening the existence of the American family, Dr. Dobson founded Focus on the Family with one employee and a once-a-week radio broadcast aired on 36 stations.

Now an international organization reaching millions of people daily, Focus on the Family is dedicated to preserving values and strengthening and encouraging families through the life-changing message of Jesus Christ.

Focus on the Family Magazines

These faith-building, character-developing publications address the interests, issues, concerns, and challenges faced by every member of your family from preschool through the senior years.

Focus on the Family
Citizen®
U.S. news issues

Focus on the Family
Clubhouse Jr.™
Ages 4 to 8

Focus on the Family
Clubhouse™
Ages 8 to 12

Breakaway®
Teen guys

Brio®
Teen girls
12 to 16

Brio & Beyond®
Teen girls
16 to 19

Plugged In®
Reviews movies,
music, TV

FOR MORE INFORMATION

 Online:
Log on to www.family.org
In Canada, log on to www.focusonthefamily.ca

 Phone:
Call toll free: (800) A-FAMILY (232-6459)
In Canada, call toll free: (800) 661-9800